Door-to-Door Ministry

The Easy Way to Make Friends for Your Church

BY

GEORGE H MARTIN

WWW.GEORGEMARTIN.ORG

Door-to-Door Ministry

THE EASY WAY TO MAKE FRIENDS FOR YOUR CHURCH

ISBN: 0615930387
ISBN: 9780615930381
Library of Congress Control Number: 2013922170
George H. Martin
12305 Chinchilla Ct. W.
Rosemount, MN 55068

Door-to-Door Ministry
The Easy Way to Make Friends for Your Church

Table of Contents

Preface

A Parable

On a dangerous seacoast where shipwrecks often occur there was once a crude little lifesaving station. The building was just a hut, and there was only one boat, but the few devoted members kept a constant watch over the sea and, with no thought for themselves, went out day and night, tirelessly searching for the lost. Many lives were saved through this wonderful little station, so that it became famous. Some of those who were saved, and various others in the surrounding area, wanted to become associated with the station and give of their time, money and effort for the support of its work. New boats were bought and new crews trained. The little lifesaving station grew.

Some of the members of the lifesaving station were unhappy that the building was so crude and poorly equipped. They felt that a more comfortable place should be provided as the first refuge for those saved from the sea. So they replaced the emergency cots with beds and put better furniture in the enlarged building. Now the lifesaving station became a popular gathering place for its members, and they decorated it beautifully and furnished it exquisitely, because they used it as a sort of club. Fewer members were now interested in going to sea on lifesaving missions, so they hired lifeboat crews to do this work. The lifesaving motif still prevailed in this club's decoration, and there was a liturgical lifeboat in the room where the club initiations were held. About this time, a large ship was wrecked off the coast, and the hired crews brought in boatloads of cold, wet, and half-drowned people. They were dirty and sick, and some of them had black skin and some had yellow skin. The beautiful new clubhouse was in chaos. So the property committee immediately had a shower house built outside the club where victims of a shipwreck could be cleaned up before coming inside.

At the next meeting, there was a split in the club membership. Most of the members wanted to stop the club's lifesaving activities, which had become unpleasant and a hindrance to the normal social life of the club. Some members insisted upon lifesaving as their primary purpose and pointed out that they were still called a lifesaving station. But they were finally voted down and told that, if they wanted to save the lives of all the various kinds of people who were shipwrecked in those waters, they could begin their own lifesaving station down the coast. They did.

At the next meeting, there was a split in the club membership. Most of the members wanted to stop the club's lifesaving activities, which had become unpleasant and a hindrance to the normal social life of the club. Some members insisted upon lifesaving as their primary purpose and pointed out that they were still called a lifesaving station. But they were finally voted down and told that, if they wanted to save the lives of all the various kinds of people who were shipwrecked in those waters, they could begin their own lifesaving station down the coast. They did.

As the years went by, the new station experienced the same changes that had occurred in the old. It evolved into a club, and yet another lifesaving station was founded. History continued to repeat itself, and if you visit that seacoast today, you will find a number of exclusive clubs along that shore. Shipwrecks are frequent in those waters but most of the people drown.

Note: The original version of this parable appeared in an article by Theodore O. Wedel, "Evangelism—The Mission of the Church to Those Outside Her Life," *The Ecumenical Review,* October 1953, p. 24. The above paraphrase of the original is by Richard Wheatcroft. It appeared in *Letter to Laymen,* May–June 1962, p.1.

Introduction

Door-to-Door Ministry: A Lifesaving Ministry

The book that you are reading is most likely not going to end up on any best-seller list. More than once, I've told people that this is "the least-read book ever published." Its narrow audience is also why it is a self-published book. The reason is fairly obvious, since this ministry is something akin to that described in the previous parable. Many existing churches were actually founded on the principles and practices described herein, but as the external focus on evangelism has sadly faded from the picture, many of our congregations have become more like clubs than mission stations.

The hope in putting this book together and making it available is that there will be enough adventurous souls who see the need and are willing to respond. I'm hopeful that more of our churches will return to their original mission.

I've included in this book many practical details related to door-to-door ministry, as well as a clear rationale for entering into this ministry, in the hope that a few teams of people will step out from their local church communities to continue the ministry of invitation. I have no doubt that there will be blessings for many in that process. As will be pointed out in this work, this life-saving activity was part of the plan of

Jesus and one of the first missionary efforts of the early disciples. Those who keep this ministry going are following in the footsteps of those first disciples.

This latest updated edition also recognizes that the times have changed since this was first written in the early 1990s. *I still believe that the methodology is relevant, however.* Observe the Jehovah Witnesses, if you will, who knock on doors still, and how the Mormons keep sending out missionaries all over the world in pairs. While I admire the commitment of those just mentioned, you will discover major and significant differences in my approach to door-to-door ministry.

The changes that I've made in this updated version involve little in terms of the basic concepts of this ministry as I first discovered it, and I definitely still stand behind the theological and Biblical concepts that I believe are foundational. Having now worked in churches where gated communities abound, and having lived in apartment complexes while doing interim work around the country, I am aware that it isn't always easy to get to everyone. It was much easier to do this work when I started a church in a fast-growing suburb. This edition recognizes that sometimes it's hard to reach some people. Even so, there are aspects of this ministry that work in all kinds of situations.

We now need to incorporate social-networking methodologies into this ministry. If you meet someone for the first time at their front door, it's now possible to continue the relationship through Facebook, Twitter, or a myriad of other social networking sites. The last twenty years have changed other ways in which we can share ideas and information. Whereas I used to bring a VHS-formatted video which told the story of our church and then showed it in someone's home on a follow-up visit, I now encourage the church to create *YouTube* videos (maybe appearing on the church's Web site) that demonstrate what life in their church looks like. That information needs to be on the door-hanger you leave with people. Maybe it's a DVD that you send as a follow-up gift to a prospect. In this new edition I also talk about the concepts of "event evangelism" in their community outreach. I've added a special chapter called "Reasons to Reach Out to Your Community," which discusses how event evangelism can be connected to door-to-door ministry.

The very idea of knocking on the door of a strange house may cause butterflies in your stomach even as you come to the end of this Introduction. You're in good company. I can assure that even if you never knock on a door as I have done, you'll find much in this book that touches on the kinds of evangelism that still can make a huge difference in your church. At the very least you'll be in a much better position to follow-up on your guests. You'll be sure to also be welcoming guests instead of having visitors to your church. Chances are that your church will be trying many different ways to be more visible and welcoming at the same time. If these kinds of things start to happen you'll find some of your old-timers, maybe those who know the stories of the early days, start to smile at the return of the "missionary spirit" that founded your church. Wouldn't that be a great outcome?

I invite you to keep reading and discover some ideas that will keep you and the members of your church constantly learning the names of more and more people who come through your doors—many of course, we hope and pray, who will stay and grow in faith in a life of service and witness to the love of God we discover in Jesus the Christ.

Chapter 1

What Was I Thinking? Standing at All Those Doors!

This book about "door-to-door" calling contains a number of surprises, and one of the first has to be the identity of its author. Most church people curious about this form of ministry would probably expect the author to stand in one of those Christian traditions with a long history of public witnessing. My roots are different. I was ordained as an Episcopal priest. I happen to have been trained in what was once considered one of our "low-church evangelical" seminaries—but even coming from that environment, no one ever talked about knocking on doors.

To be sure, my willingness to knock on strangers' doors did not characterize the early parts of my ministry. Let me tell you briefly how this evolved. I am one of those clergy who happened to attend seminary right out of college. When I was 24 years old, I was ordained a deacon in the Episcopal Church and six months later was ordained a priest. My ministry began as an associate in a suburban congregation, where I learned a model of ministry that would serve me well for the next 20 years. Like many others, I had a ministry rooted, grounded, and centered in the life of the congregation. I was their priest and their pastor. Ministry meant serving the people in those particular congregations. To look at my daily calendar through those 20 years is to analyze a continual series of meetings, personal visits with parishioners in their homes or at the hospital, and various worship services. To be sure, there were community events and activities, but they were more often than not church-related. You would not find in those early years too many occasions in which I purposely sought out people in order to invite them into the church. My focus for ministry during most of that time was on those who were already gathered into the flock. Those were the years when we assumed that our church buildings attracted people! The clergy were pastors to those who self-selected their own church.

I am sure a semantic analysis of my preaching during those early years would also likely find only a few occurrences of the word "evangelism." Church historians, when looking back at this period of church history, will surely note that the word "evangelism" was mostly absent from the vocabulary of mainstream Christian language systems until sometime in the late 1970s. I was no different. Throughout the 1980s, the "E word," as some called it, began to appear more and more, until finally various church traditions, including the Episcopal Church, declared the 1990s the "decade of evangelism." Whether or not these churches have actually turned the corner on evangelism is debatable, but it is still notable that many mainstream churches now use the noun "evangelism" or the adjective "evangelistic" with some frequency, even if we don't fully know what it means. More than once I've heard people wonder if these terms still really mean "door-to-door ministry."

My personal history of ministry has seen me make the shift from an internal to an external focus of ministry. I think it began in 1975 when I was called to serve as the pastor of a congregation in Minneapolis that seemed to have left its better days in the past. As I looked around the area where the church served, however, I saw many younger couples and families moving into the large homes that dominated that part of the city. These homes weren't filled with the same number of children they once contained, but that was because families were smaller, and many of these young couples were buying a house first and only later starting to think about having children. I worried about the declining size of my congregation and its increasing age, and I wondered how we might start to attract these young adults into the church. At that time, I had no idea that it might be helpful if I went visiting.

I chose **advertising** as the best method to reach people who were not attending church. Back in 1978, with the help of some highly creative people, we developed a series of print ads for the congregation I was serving. The ads actually worked. New people started to visit and join our congregation, and many of them told us that our ads helped them to start thinking about making that first visit. Working with advertising people, I started to sense the power inherent in strong media messages. Using the right words and visuals gave us advertising that raised the visibility of our church in the community. The same advertising led people to make an initial visit to the church.

One of the many ads created by the Church
Ad Project. These are now out-of-print.

The ministry of the Church Ad Project was born out of that advertising effort. It is a ministry that is no longer in business, I'm sad to report. Even so, I'm proud of the work we created and pleased with the good that these creative ads accomplished in the 25 years during which this project flourished.

As this book demonstrates, I have grown in my understanding of evangelism. Advertising, like that which was promoted by the Church Ad Project, has an important role to play in the ministry of the church, *but it can never take the place of other ministries of outreach.* No matter how we use advertising, it will always be less personal than other forms of witness and invitation. The typology in Chart 1 (See the next chapter) points out some significant differences between various forms of evangelism.

That chart also shows that door-to-door ministry is the method that requires the least amount of technology. It may take courage to make the first call, but knocking on a door requires little technological expertise—feet willing to walk, a hand that knocks or pushes a door bell, and a smile, and that's about it. Many other evangelistic tools—effective in their own ways—often suffer in comparison because they are either less personal or more costly. The same chart also shows a direct correlation between levels of technology and degree of cost, because many methods requiring technological expertise are by definition often more costly. The one exception on this list is social networking, which I believe needs to be incorporated into our understanding of door-to-door ministry.

Famous Last Words

I need to get back to the story that led me to start knocking on doors, because it relates to some famous last words I spoke in reference to "door-to-door" ministry. In my naiveté, I thought that, of all the methods of evangelism available to me, the least effective would be knocking on doors. In 1986 we had started a new church and I was happy to be asked to plant this church. I had the support of a wonderful committee in the diocese, which gave me plenty of encouragement. On the committee was one man who kept asking me to knock on doors, and here is what I said to him: "I do not need to go door-to-door. It's like looking for a needle in a haystack." You are reading the manual that says that I ended up eating those words.

This new Episcopal church was started in a fast-growing suburb south of Minneapolis and St. Paul. Nearby, a young Lutheran pastor was also starting a church. While our two traditions are fairly close in terms of theology, the cultural situation was different. The Lutheran pastor had what I considered to be a clear advantage, since so many people in the population already claimed a Lutheran heritage. He was looking for "Lutherans" who were far more numerous and therefore, presumably, easier to find. I, on the other hand, was looking for those supposedly rare and difficult-to-discover "Episcopalians." Hardly ever did I stop to question these presumptions. It turned out that I was to seek those who simply were curious and who didn't have a church home, no matter what identity they may or may not have claimed for themselves.

At the time, the Lutherans had a better strategy for planting a church, since they required that the church planter knock on a certain number of doors. My friend was expected to make a minimum of 4,000 calls, and that is what he did in getting that church started. I thought that I didn't need to bother with a single call, but was I ever wrong!

Those more astute in terms of evangelistic potential may be surprised at my narrow-sighted approach to new church development. At the time, I thought we were starting a new Episcopal church in order to reach the Episcopalians moving into the area. That actually was the same kind of premise that other new church developers were using, including my friend, the Lutheran pastor. There was one major difference, however. His supervisor mandated door-to-door calling as part of his work in the first year or so of his ministry. Observing his ministry from my sociological perspective, it made sense to me that my fellow-pastor would be out looking for Lutherans. At least one out of four people in the area belonged to the Lutheran Church. By contrast, Episcopalians made up 1% or 2% of the population and I thought it would be a waste of my time to look for them. The proverbial "needle in a haystack" came to mind, and I felt that I should be making better use of my time. So much for my understanding of evangelism!

Then I had to face reality. After nine months of worship, the new congregation I had started wasn't growing very fast, and I decided to ask my Lutheran pastor friend about his calling. He told me a few of the basic methods that he followed and actually encouraged me to give this form of calling a try. I can remember to this day how I felt on that day in late April 1987 when I made my first call. Like many a caller before and since, I prayed hard as I stood at that first door. In my case, I prayed that nobody would be home! Thankfully, the Lord answered my prayer at the first two doors. Just when I thought that this calling was a breeze, I found myself face-to-face with my first real person at the door. From that first visit a full-blown calling ministry emerged and I even became someone teaching others about this ministry. Things have changed so much that it didn't take long for me to actually be disappointed when no one came to the door. My belief in this ministry now leads me to commend this form of ministry to all kinds of Christians.

Since that first call, I have made thousands of calls. I've certainly had days when I thought the work was producing few results. There have also been funny moments along the way and, I am happy to say, only a few mean dogs. Only a few people were upset that I had called on them. The reception that I have received (and that I think you can receive) is far better than you can imagine. Door-to-door ministry, though it may seem old-fashioned and maybe out-of-date, is actually one of the most productive and satisfying aspects of ministry, especially if you follow some basic guidelines involving respect for others and their beliefs.

The book you are reading contains a great deal of advice that I learned in the process of making over 14,000 calls when starting a new church. As you'll discover along the way I didn't see my role as making converts—*I was there to make friends and to meet people.* With that goal in mind, I chose my calling times carefully in order to maximize the possibility that people would be home and be receptive to a short visit. Even though I also had something to offer, I tried to remember that I brought along my ears— sometimes the best gift I had to offer was simply to listen to someone. I also learned that every call I made was an "interruption" and that another gift I gave was to not stay too long—at least not on that first visit. You will find many insights into this method in the pages that follow.

Naturally, one of the most obvious blessings were the people who joined the new congregation as a direct result of this calling. I saw people take the first steps in a spiritual life as a result of my invitation. I baptized the children of those whom I had invited, and welcomed adults to faith through baptism. Other adults, as a result of my calling, were confirmed and received into our church family. Many of those who came made public vows to follow Christ, and they came again and again to the communion rail to say "yes" to Jesus living in their lives.

I was able to count many as members of the new church as a result of my door-to-door ministry. I was also aware of others who came, sometimes with great hesitation, but who then became committed and faithful members of the church only to move far away, and then, as if to confirm all that the initial call meant, they would find another church. (Sometimes I did this door-to-door calling, as it were, to help other churches! In reality it's better to understand this spiritually as the way the Holy Spirit loves to work in our lives.) At one point, at least 20% of the families on our parish list had been found through this door-to-door ministry. At any given time, we also had record of hundreds of households that we considered active prospects because of door-to-door conversations.

When I left the new church I had started (that was in 1999), attendance after 14 years was averaging 320 at two services. The mailing list at the time included over 400 identified prospects we'd found in our door-to-door ministry.

There was also the ripple effect that took place when the newest members of our church invited their friends to attend church with them. The newest members in your church always do the best job of evangelizing others.

I've often been surprised at the results that this kind of calling can have in the lives of people. One of my daughters phoned me after she had spent a few weeks working for a new supervisor in her advertising agency. My daughter said, "Dad, you won't believe it, but you've met my supervisor." When she told me the name of her supervisor, it didn't register.

I said that I hadn't ever met her. "Oh yes, you have," my daughter said. "She remembers that you called on her a couple of times at her home in Eagan." I later checked our computer records and, sure enough, I had called on this woman and her family on two occasions. The last call had been made more than a year earlier, but this woman still remembered me and our church. I had only considered her having a modest level of interest in finding a church. Based on what my daughter told me about her supervisor, I placed her back on the prospect mailing list for our church. I wrote her a personal note and decided to make another visit, believing that, in God's time, she may start attending church. I don't know if she might have come after I left that pastorate. Maybe she found another church. What I learned over the years is to know that the outcome of the calling is out of my hands, but never outside the work of the Holy Spirit.

Immediate satisfaction and positive feedback were certainly not part of my early experience in making calls. I'll never forget asking my Lutheran pastor friend about my early disappointment with my calling ministry. I told him that I had started to discover a number of potential prospects and that a few of these people seemed genuinely interested in our church. But after calling for two months, I hadn't seen even one new family show up at church as a result of this calling. I wondered what I was doing wrong. Perhaps there was something amiss with my brochure. The Lutheran pastor simply said, "Oh, I forgot to tell you something about doing this. You have to go back and visit your prospects again."

It was a message that hit me like a ton of bricks. I had just started to become accustomed to making the first visit, and now I was receiving advice that I had to return. "What would I say?" I asked myself. I had worked out some things to say on the first visit, but what excuse would I use for the second visit? In teaching others this method, I discovered this is a common concern.

Here's what I really learned: **the payoff is in the follow-up visit!** It also turned out that the follow-up visits weren't as difficult as I imagined they might be. There is much more about this aspect of the ministry in this workbook because the strength of this, and perhaps all ministry, is found in the relationships and friendships that are formed. To be sure, a few people and households will come after a single initial visit. Every now and then I would actually find, much to my surprise, someone with some background in the Episcopal Church who had recently moved into the area, and who was hoping to find a church like ours. It helped if I caught them within a few weeks of their move. One factor in moving is that many people fall out of the habit of coming to church. Finding a new church isn't what every new resident in your town is trying to do as they settle into their new home. Just remember, finding like-minded birds isn't what this ministry is all about.

There is another aspect to this ministry that is extremely rewarding, but it is hard to quantify. The spiritual dimension of this ministry is mysteriously present. I've stood on so many doorsteps and have said so many prayers. As I walked away from a door, for example, where I saw someone who looked depressed or worried, I've offered those prayers in which I say, "God, I don't know what's going on there, but let your Spirit hover over them."

Most calls bring some kind of smile. I can't begin to count the number of friendly, common exchanges I made while calling. I have no idea how many times I've said, "That's great. I think it's wonderful that you have a church." Strangely, more often than not, I'm thanked for having come to their door. Can you imagine that? After interrupting someone from something so I can ask them if they have a church, they end up thanking me! The more skeptical reader is naturally not going to believe me at this point, but this happened quite frequently. I'd love to go with you, into a neighborhood near your church, and let you see the same response happen over and over again.

How does this ministry actually encourage people in their own spiritual lives? It is a two-way street. It is probably understandable to the first-time caller that this ministry leads to the prayer that I first prayed, "Oh, let no one be home!" There is, after all, a certain kind of fear and anxiety associated with this calling. After a while, my prayer continued but it was different. The prayer was no longer about what I needed, but it became a petition asking for God's blessing to be with the people being visited. "God bless this house." While those words may often be found on a brass door-knocker, they are better said by the one knocking on the door.

Please consider as well many of the less-tangible results of Door-to-door Ministry which may be difficult to quantify, but which I learned clearly happen:

- Greater visibility of your church in its community
- A residual feeling of good-will from those you've met—many who thanked you for calling on them! Imagine that?
- And that seed planted, the invitation made, which might sit in the ground for a while, and eventually lead people seek out a church, maybe in time of crisis or need, or simply because of their questions. That's where the Holy Spirit is working!

I hope all who read this, even if only a very few in actual numbers, understand that the main thing is to make calls in the context of a welcoming spirit that exudes love and joy. I was never knocking on a door to make a judgment about someone's religious faith or lack thereof, but only to represent Christ in a way that might give God the glory. If my call let my church have greater visibility, that was fine—and I might even find someone who would come to visit. The outcome of the call was never in my hands. I was there to smile and to invite, and to know that the outcome was in God's hands.

The Other Door at Which to Stand: The Church Door[1]

I would be terribly remiss in this introduction if I didn't let you see where I also stood every Sunday before worship began. During the last 25 years of active pastoral ministry, I made it a point to stand outside

---

[1] "I Stand at the Door" is also the title of a prose-poem written by the Rev Samuel Shoemaker (1893-1963), the Episcopal priest from Pittsburgh, PA who was influential in the early days of Alcoholics Anonymous. Shoemaker was credited by Bill W. for helping influence the writing of the 12 Steps of AA. This poem captures the spirit of a pastor who stands at the door to welcome people inside where they may find rest and comfort for their souls. One link to this poem is at: http://www.thejaywalker.com/pages/shoemaker.html

the main church doors, wherever it was that I was serving, and welcome people as they came to church.

As a pastor in the Episcopal Church, that meant standing outside in my vestments. We Episcopalians like to dress up in funny clothes. I just added something many clergy forget to wear on a Sunday morning. I wore a nametag on my vestments—with easy-to-read letters. One line simply had my name, "George Martin," and below it in somewhat smaller letters was the word "Pastor."

If a new person was coming because of that call I made, there I was at the door to the church. They'd welcomed me and now I was welcoming them. Even if you don't engage in door-to-door ministry, I highly commend the practice of the leadership of the church taking an active and visible role in welcoming people at the door, and doing that on a consistent Sunday-to-Sunday basis.

If you wanted to avoid having me welcome you to the church, you had to arrive late. Otherwise, I was the one who opened the door for our first-time guests, and in some powerful instances, it followed upon my visit to the home where they had first welcomed me.

This teaching book discusses many of the practical aspects of going door-to-door, but deep down there is the metaphor of someone opening a door to a deeper relationship with God which, thankfully, many of us know and celebrate through worship and fellowship in the church. I know that being outside those main church doors on a Sunday wasn't something I was expected to do and neither does door-to-door ministry fit into most job descriptions for clergy and, I might add, regular members of our churches. Nonetheless, I'm offering you two powerful pictures that can speak volumes about God's desire to be known by all. I stood at their door so that they might come to the door of God's house.

Chapter 2

Evangelism Strategies: A Typology

An emphasis on evangelism started to dominate the discussion and agenda of many churches in the latter part of the 20th century, even those churches that previously would have been uncomfortable using such a designation. The word "evangelism" or "evangelistic" even began being incorporated into the official names chosen for a church. A merger of two large Lutheran church bodies led to the formation, for example, of the Evangelical Lutheran Church of America, otherwise known by its initials, ELCA. The last decade of the 20th century was even declared by Lutherans, Episcopalians, and others to be the Decade of Evangelism. To be sure, when the new century dawned and that decade ended, there was serious doubt in the minds of some that much evangelism had actually been accomplished. (Many of the same churches starting to emphasize evangelism had seen declining numbers.) At the same time, there was clear evidence from around the world that evangelistic activity was having great success, particularly in other parts of the world.

For all the talk about evangelism, however, we still don't have common agreement on the meaning of the word, and we have even less agreement on evangelistic methods. Given the tremendous variety within the Christian family, we shouldn't be too surprised to find great variation in the way the Gospel is proclaimed. For some Christians, the proclamation is meant to lead to a singular once-in-a-lifetime identifiable decision point. Others approach evangelism more in terms of a process, or a set of practices that lead toward membership and affiliation, as well as participation in the life of a local church community. Sometimes evangelism is equated with the numerical growth of the church, while in other instances certain internal focus classes or programs are identified as evangelistic.

When we look at the range of evangelistic tools or methods, they range from the obvious ones like an altar call to the more subtle ones like an invitation to attend church. Many people assume that door-to-door ministry is in the first category, interpreting this as a blatant or more coercive attempt to persuade people to become Christians. In my experience teaching about this ministry, I've discovered that many people have this negative picture in mind. Lest the reader wonder, let me assure you that you won't find advice in this manual about making a convert in the context of an initial visit. A theme, that I hope is consistent, is that this ministry is primarily invitational, not confrontational!

The idea of door-to-door ministry is often associated with groups like the Mormons or Jehovah Witnesses, who may seem to press for a decision. Personally, I don't think these two groups deserve the harsh judgments rendered to them for their dedication in trying to communicate their faith and make invitations to others. Even so, I must admit that many people have, unfortunately, come to a negative opinion about this method of evangelism as a result of some callers with motives that appear questionable. Along with all the jokes about the guy who walks around with an "end of the world" sign, there is a common assumption that those who go door-to-door have somehow run out of options for communicating the message. In the eye of the skeptical believer, going door-to-door seems to be the method of last resort. It isn't!

My hope is that those reading this workbook will be a little more receptive to thinking about the positive ways the door-to-door ministry can be an effective and important tool to use alongside other evangelical methods. In my experience this is a form of ministry and outreach that can be a positive and productive experience, not just for those who do the calling but for those we meet in our neighborhoods.

A little healthy skepticism, however, is also in order. Ubiquitous in nearly every city in America (to say nothing of their presence in nearly every country in the world), more than 60,000 young men each year serve as Mormon missionaries. We know that their method includes knocking on doors. What most people do not realize is that these missionaries rarely reap a great harvest. Overall, however, the Mormon Church is growing much faster than almost any other religion. According to an article I found almost 10 years ago, the Mormon Church increased by over 225% in a 30-year period. That growth, however, wasn't due only to their door-knocking methods, since on average each missionary sent out could claim fewer than five converts. That report noted that 60,000 missionaries recorded 274,000 converts—a lot of door knocking to reap that result.

My experience with this ministry, along with what I've learned from others, tells a quite different story. To be sure, I called in an area where people also heard from Mormons and from Jehovah Witnesses. The church I was planting was in a suburb of Minneapolis–St. Paul where there was already a fairly high degree of religious affiliation. On average, over 70% of the people I met claimed some association with a church, synagogue, mosque, or Buddhist temple. I also found that about 1% of the population were Mormon. Even fewer were Jehovah Witnesses, and ironically they were often the least receptive, at least in terms of being willing to have a conversation.

Why bother to call in an area where so many people are already involved in a religious community? My answer to that question is that, out of every hundred houses where I called and found someone home, I would usually walk away with 10 to 20 prospects—meaning there was at least *some* interest in having a church home, even if it wasn't one that I represented. As I discovered, it was at least easy, relatively speaking, to develop a prospect list.

The reader will discover that door-to-door ministry is a method connected in some powerful ways to a wide range of evangelistic tools. It is just one of the tools—and, in my opinion, one of the foundational tools in the total package. As I recommend this approach, I can assure you that some delightful surprises are waiting for those who do the calling. At the very least, please realize that the prospect list which emerges from this process is like knowing where the gold is buried. You still have to dig for the gold, and even after that, it's not the kind of gold that can be turned into jewelry, but at least you know where to find it.

I must emphasize, in an unequivocal way, that I do not advocate a method that is confrontational. To be perfectly clear, this is a form of "invitational evangelism." Far from receiving a negative response or being discouraged after doing this calling, if it happens according to the guidelines found herein, I can assure you that you will find real enjoyment in meeting the people in your community. I can promise you that a great many of the people you meet are actually going to thank you for calling on them. The residual effects of this ministry will remain for a very long time. You will be planting a great deal of goodwill in your community if you take this open and more joyful approach to this ministry. Be assured that your greatest satisfaction will come from the relationships that emerge—not only with the friends you find joining you in your church, but *with the friends you have in the larger community who know about your church.*

Framing Door-to-Door Ministry in a Larger Context

The concept of doing ministry in the language and ways appropriate to your culture and your times can be traced back to the ministry of St. Paul, who said,

> To the Jews I became as a Jew, in order to win Jews. To those under the law I became as one under the law (though I myself am not under the law) so that I might win those under the law. To those outside the law I became as one outside the law (though I am not free from

God's law but am under Christ's law) so that I might win those outside the law. To the weak I became weak, so that I might win the weak. I have become all things to all people, that I might by all means save some. I do it all for the sake of the gospel, so that I may share in its blessings. (1 Corinthians 9:20–23)

Sometimes this is called "contextual missionary strategy." It simply means using the tools that are available in your time. In our time, marked by many advances in technology and electronics, we have access to large numbers of people all at once through the Internet or through mass marketing. We can find friends on Facebook almost instantaneously. And, just as people have always wanted (for the most part) to live next door to their neighbors, most of us live in some kind of neighborhood, whether one of houses or some apartment complex.

The average church with a modest budget has to be realistic about what it can do to reach those in its neighborhood, and those who may live at some distance, because we know that some members are willing to travel several miles to come to the church they love and serve. We may belong to a denomination that might conceivably have the resources to do mass marketing, but on a practical level our use of television might be restricted to the free cable ads available on the local cable network. Most congregations will have at least some younger adults who would know how to create a webpage and a Facebook presence for the church, and that is one skill that requires some technological expertise.

The chart below shows a scale of marketing and advertising options, ranging from tools that use technology to those that require great training and expertise, as well as the financial resources needed. On the other hand, many of the mass marketing efforts, which by definition reach a lot of people, often do so in an impersonal way. Upon hearing a recorded phone message, for example, in the middle of an election cycle, most of us will simply hang up, knowing that it's simply a recorded voice. Very few of us will spend time on the phone if we can't at least hear a real voice.

The chart below shows that door-to-door ministry is a method that requires little technology, because the only thing you have to do is ring the doorbell or knock on the door. It is also the most personal form of ministry in this toolbox. Other evangelical tools suffer in comparison because they are less personal, more costly, or require greater technological expertise.

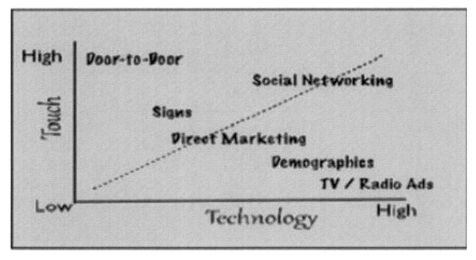

Chart 1 : Comparing Evangelistic Strategies

Most likely, the best kind of evangelism isn't even listed on this chart. Imagine two friends having a cup of coffee together at their local Starbucks, and one of them says, "I heard a fantastic sermon in church this past Sunday. It was as though it had been written just for me." It's just a conversation, but that statement is an opening for all kinds of questions to follow. It's an opportunity for a witness that truly is "high-touch and low-tech."

At the other extreme is a television commercial, such as the United Methodist Church used in their "Open hands, Open hearts, Open minds" campaign around 2009. The method was reaching thousands of people, perhaps millions, and was using what is called *the law of large numbers*. It was also a method requiring a large budget. And it was an example of a method, not without some effectiveness, best defined as "low-touch, high-tech."

Perhaps the best-known industry that uses a combination of both approaches is the automobile industry. A great deal of money is spent on television and print advertising, and yet they still rely on salespeople inside each dealership at the actual point-of-sale. I once read that Japanese auto dealers go one step further: Many of them go door-to-door.

My emphasis upon door-to-door ministry has always included a number of other tools that are also effective for reaching people. For example, every one of the prospects identified in our door-to-door ministry started to receive a free one-year subscription to the church's newsletter, and also received postcards that advertised special services. In one sense, we were using door-to-door ministry to create a more refined direct mail list, one we couldn't even afford to buy, let alone find.

Door-to-door ministry was also a form of demographic research in our community that gave us not only an accurate percentage of those who did not attend church (or claim membership in one), but one that collected their addresses as well so that we could follow up either with more visits (an essential part of the process) or additional information by mail.

I recommend a planned approach to door-to-door ministry in which your church keeps visiting neighborhoods—probably the ones you determine where you will find a receptive audience—and that you keep visiting them until you've met a number of people that seems sufficient. You'll never reach everyone. We know that. Next? Well there are other neighborhoods to visit!

In the door-to-door methodology explained here, the emphasis is on completing the follow-up in a neighborhood until a contact has been made at most of the homes. I do not advocate calling again at a home where people have indicated they belong to a church. I also made it a point to respect the person who told me that they weren't interested in finding a church.

Setting those two groups aside I, nonetheless, always had a list of prospects, and a list that kept growing, as long as we kept knocking on doors. Since a personal relationship has been established with someone in every unchurched household, the presumption is that we continue, at least for a while, some kind of follow-up with most of the prospective members.

As mentioned earlier, there are different ways in which we receive information and make decisions. We all differ in how we would respond to a personal invitation, a newspaper announcement, a written invitation, or a need for pastoral counseling. As you learn more about this particular method in this workbook, be mindful of the need to have other tools inside your church's evangelistic toolbox.

Chapter 3

A Biblical Foundation for Door-to-Door Ministry

When I started looking more closely at the scriptural foundations for this ministry, I was led to investigate the stories in Luke's Gospel where Jesus sends out missionaries. There are two related events found in Luke 9 and 10 in which Jesus sent out people to preach and heal in his name. The two stories are not only intimately related to each other,[2] but I think they contain ideas and themes found throughout the whole of the Luke-Acts story. The question in the mind of the author is **how will others know** of what God has done in the life of Jesus who is the Christ? In a very real sense, we can understand **all** of Luke and Acts as an answer to that question. The missionary mandate lies just below the surface throughout Luke's Gospel. It is a mandate that first comes directly to the surface in many places, but particularly when Jesus sends out his disciples in Luke 9:2. Soon after, there is a second missionary effort involving 70 other disciples in Luke 10:1.

---

[2] The initial ideas for this chapter came from Joseph C. Aldrich, author of *Gentle Persuasion: Creative ways to introduce your friends to Christ*. In a chapter titled "Can You Bake a Cherry Pie," Aldrich discusses the relationship between Luke 9:2 and 10:1, with the main goal of encouraging personal evangelism.

In reading any particular story in Luke-Acts, I have found it valuable to keep asking myself how that story relates to the larger picture offered by the author. My presumption, in fact, is that the author always has the larger view in mind. The stories as we have them are not isolated events that were haphazardly connected. I will show in detail, for example, how the two "sending out" stories are carefully woven together. Using a truly wide-angle lens, I even believe that Luke-Acts is telling us that, as a result of the Jesus experience, the locus of Christian faith has shifted more to a foundation in the homes where God's people dwell. I call this "Home Theology" because I think it is such a distinctive feature of the Gospel of Luke.

I have used the ideas in this chapter in nearly every conference when I have taught people about door-to-door ministry. In my experience most Christians who are willing to consider the possibilities of this ministry appreciate seeing the Biblical foundations for this kind of missionary endeavor. Those using this book to train others are advised to adapt this chapter as needed. At the very least, I suggest that those going out look at the key elements of the story in Luke 10:1–8. If there is plenty of time for teaching the Biblical foundations for this ministry, then I encourage people to use all of the ideas in this chapter.

What is Home Theology?

As far as I know, this is a unique term that I have coined. It began with my study of the material in Luke 9:1 to 10:8, but then I began to look further afield in Luke. Luke begins with the story of Zechariah, who is serving in the house of the Lord. After receiving a message from the angel Gabriel telling him that he will at long last have a son, Zechariah loses his ability to speak. But then (1:23) he goes home. Not too long after that, this home is mentioned again when Mary, pregnant with Jesus, comes to visit her relative, Elizabeth, the wife of Zechariah.

The Gospel of Luke[3] ends with a story about Paul who was living under arrest in Rome. The circumstances of his arrest were such that he was allowed to live in his own dwelling, and from this place he welcomed visitors. It was—as the last verse tells us—a place used for "proclaiming the kingdom of God and teaching about the Lord Jesus Christ with all boldness and without hindrance." (Acts 28:16)

How interesting it is that Luke-Acts begins in the temple and ends in some long-forgotten house in Rome where Paul is under house arrest. In the temple, Zechariah has lost his ability to speak, while at the end, Paul speaks freely about Jesus Christ to all who come. The temple, which was at the center of the world in terms of Hebraic spirituality, had continued beyond ethnic boundaries (at least in the mind of the Luke-Acts author) by the message of Jesus, which stayed alive in a community that gathered in people's homes. In those homes they told the stories and shared the bread and wine, as they had been taught to do at the Last Supper.

There is something powerful and significant taking place throughout Luke-Acts as we discover the Jesus community spreading its message of salvation. The image given in Acts 1:8 is something like the ripples in a pond when a stone is thrown into the water. "You will be my witnesses in Jerusalem, in all Judea and Samaria, and to the ends of the earth." In terms of a Jewish audience for this gospel, the message would be that this missionary effort begins at the center of their world and then moves out to the furthest fringes. In other words, the witnessing is to begin at home and then it moves beyond—way beyond the borders of their world. The author of Luke-Acts accordingly follows this pattern as the story begins in the temple in Jerusalem and symbolically ends up in Rome, the political power that was reaching to the ends of the earth. The story begins in the religious home of the Jewish people and concludes in the political home of Roman power. Even using the broadest

---

[3] Please note that in speaking of "The Gospel of Luke" in this context, I am seeing Luke and the Acts of the Apostles as one single gospel. It's clear from the introduction in the Gospel itself that the story doesn't end with the resurrection of Jesus. In the rest of the chapter I'll reference the entire work a "Luke-Acts", but that doesn't carry the same weight as thinking of all of it as a single Gospel story, which I believe was the original intent of the author.

kind of metaphors, we can see that the gospel story is a form of "Home Theology."

The author of the gospel may have had a grand outline in mind, but filled in the story with specific names, places, and events. The author of Luke-Acts was probably grounded in some of the classical philosophical schools of thought, but was also far more practical and down to earth in presenting the story of Jesus Christ. There is no phrase here, for example, like "the word became flesh" as there is in John's Gospel. Instead, Jesus joins the human community in a stable. From that point on, the story is found rooted in specific communities. Ironically, one of the first stories of rejection, when the good news didn't find any roots, takes place in Nazareth, the hometown of Jesus. In Luke 4:29, the townspeople actually attempt to murder him, but he flees.

Even as he fled, however, Jesus went somewhere. Luke tells us that Jesus went to Capernaum and that he taught there on the Sabbath. While in that town, Jesus healed a man with an unclean spirit and Peter's mother-in-law, among many others who are not named. Let us not forget he's in her house or Peter's, as well. An interesting exchange took place on the next day when Jesus was about to leave. The townspeople wanted Jesus to stay, but he said to them, "I must proclaim the good news of the kingdom of God to the other cities also; for I was sent for this purpose." (Luke 4:43) The words of Jesus here are not unique to Luke, since they are also found in Mark 1:38; but in the context of Luke's Gospel, the words take on added meaning. By adding the story of the early church to the gospel, we see the way in which many Christian communities sprang to life in town after town. Luke began by telling about the life of Christ but, as his narrative shows, Luke knew that the story of faith involved particular individuals who joined the community of believers. For Luke, it appears that it isn't sufficient to tell the story of Jesus finding a home in this world if there aren't homes in the various communities of Luke's world that also give a spiritual home to Jesus.

There are many interesting examples throughout Luke-Acts where a "home" or a "house" plays a key role in the unfolding story of either Jesus or the early Jesus community. It is important to note, for example, that Jesus was born in Bethlehem, a town name that means "House of Bread." This fact was certainly known to the author of Luke-Acts. Earlier I made reference to Jesus being in the home of Peter. Consider also some of the other homes Jesus entered:

Some of the homes Jesus entered in Luke's gospel

- Levi, the tax collector's house (Luke 5:29)
- The Pharisee's house—sinful woman anoints Jesus (Luke 7:36–50)
- The home of Jairus (Luke 8:40–56)
- The home of Martha and Mary (Luke 10:38–42)
- Another house of a Pharisee (Luke 14:1–14)
- The home of Zacchaeus (Luke 19:1–9)
- The house for Passover celebration (Luke 22:7–38)

There are many more references to a house that are found in the parables and teachings of Jesus in Luke's Gospel. Consider some of the following:

Luke: Home references in some parables and teachings

- David who ate bread in the temple (Luke 6:1–5)
- The house built on rock (Luke 6:46–49)
- Look at those living in palaces (Luke 7:24–28)
- Lamp on lampstand (in a house) (Luke 8:16–18)
- To the house of a friend at midnight (Luke 11:5–13)
- House divided cannot stand (Luke 11:14–23)
- Master finds watchful servants (Luke 12:34–40)
- The parable of the great dinner (Luke 14:15–24)
- The parable of the lost coin (Luke 15:8–10)
- The parable of the prodigal and his brother (Luke 15:11–32)
- The rich man and Lazarus (Luke 16:19–30)

The above list of stories involving a home is not exhaustive. There are also stories in which a home is implicitly assumed, but not overtly mentioned. The "Parable of the Dishonest Manager" (Luke 16:1–13) is a story, for example, that clearly involves a manager who is in charge of a house, and who fears losing his own happy home. The "Parable of the Pharisee and the Tax Collector" should be understood as taking place in another kind of home as it takes place in the Jerusalem temple, the home of God. Since the main purpose of this writing is not to do an extensive analysis of all the ways in which the concept of "home" is used in Luke, I have only pointed to some of the more obvious examples in order to show how important this concept is to the author of this gospel. In terms of this emphasis on door-to-door ministry, I find it most helpful to concentrate on two closely connected passages in which Jesus sends his followers out to preach and heal. For the rest of this chapter, therefore, I will be concentrating on these two stories.

Two Stories of Sending Out

The reader should take time to read the two stories in Luke 9 and 10 that are under discussion. They are printed in the Appendix of the book.

This in-depth study will reveal some interesting and important ideas that were at the heart of the early missionary effort of the first Christians, as recorded in Luke-Acts. To be sure, each of these two stories is a missionary effort organized by Jesus, but I am inclined to believe that these two stories also tell us something about the experience of the early Christians in giving witness to Jesus. As I read parts of Luke's Gospel, I think we need to be aware of the fact that three different things may be happening with the same stories. First, the story may on the surface be faithfully reporting an event that actually happened during the ministry of Jesus. In the second place, the same story may be telling us something about the early Christian community, simply by virtue of the fact that this was a story remembered and cherished. It may be the case that elements of the early church experience have touched and colored the telling of the story. Finally, the story itself may contain moralistic, ethical, or practical advice that allows the author to be a preacher or teacher. It is possible that all three elements occur within a given story, or it may be that only one aspect is central in the mind of the author.

When I look at Luke 9 and 10, I see aspects of the story that relate to all three levels of analytical study. I have no doubt that something in the way of a missionary effort actually occurred during the ministry of Jesus. At the same time, I think it possible to see a few of the ways in which the early Christians might have used these stories to bolster their own efforts to share the Gospel. Finally, I think there are some practical, sensible ideas contained in these stories that belong to the world of practical wisdom, which somehow transcend time. I daresay that some of the principles will be found in the practical instructions in this workbook.

In choosing to focus on Luke's two episodes involving missionary efforts, I'm not ignoring that Matthew tells a single story (Matthew 10:5–15).[4] What I find most interesting is that Luke's layout of stories between the two times that he sends out disciples (first 12 and then 70) includes a set of stories that frame what I think are the two key missionary questions.

Comparing Luke 9 and 10

When we look at Luke 9 and 10, at the two stories related to sending missionaries, we see many similarities and many differences. The similarities are as follows:

1. Jesus takes the leadership.
2. They are to proclaim a message about the Kingdom of God.
3. Prohibitions about what to take; only taking a bag is forbidden in both.

---

[4] Note that Matthew 10:1–15 is almost an exact parallel with most of the instructions given by Jesus in Luke 9–10. Matthew, however, doesn't tell us that the disciples actually went out. They are also given the title "apostles" before the instructions are given. The distinctive phrase, "The harvest is plentiful but the laborers are few…," is also unique to Luke. The same story appears in Mark 6:6-13 but with the fewest details in comparison with Luke and Matthew.

4. The disciples are to look for a house to stay in.
5. If not welcomed, shake the dust off your feet.

What is striking is that the differences between the two stories far outweigh the similarities. The study of the differences is made somewhat more difficult by the way Luke uses Matthew 10:5–15, where the twelve are sent out. It appears that this event was probably in the common document, often referred to as "Q," which the two gospel authors shared. The second story, where 70 are sent out, seems to be unique to Luke. But Luke didn't report the sending out of the disciples exactly as Matthew did. Luke, in fact, disperses parts of the single Matthew story into his two stories.

What is clear is that the unique parts of Luke's sense of mission, as they emerge through the second missionary effort, are found partly in the added number of details and spoken words when 70 disciples are sent out. The first missionary effort takes up only six verses, while the second telling requires at least twelve verses—and a few more if we include the section that involves the return of the 70 from their journey (see Luke 10:17–20).

I've learned to read Luke not only with my eye on the details of the stories, but with special attention to the linkages between the stories. If we look at the way the narratives are organized, we can grow in our understanding of the author's intent. I believe, in fact, that Luke carefully placed these two stories in a larger context. The first sending out doesn't immediately lead to the second event. Consider, then, the logic of the order in which the author has linked the stories together. It seems as if Luke creates a kind of sandwich linking the two events in which missionaries are sent out in the name of Jesus. In between the two missions are different sayings, miracles, and healings. There is an internal order and logic to all these pericopes because they seem to alternate between two questions. The two questions are: "Who is Jesus?" and "What does it mean to follow Jesus?" The following chart shows the way in which a story answering one of the questions leads to another story dealing with the opposite question.

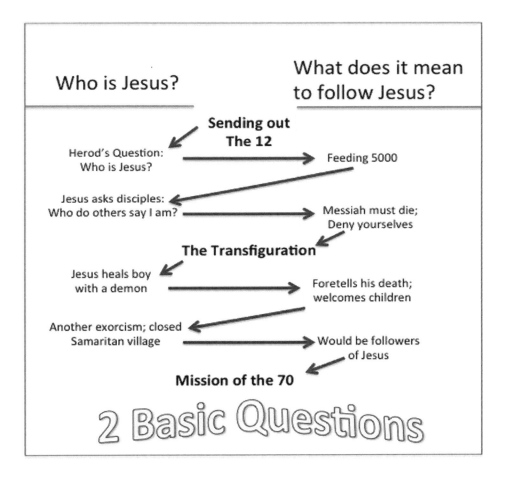

This chart illustrates, the way the author of Luke linked the two stories in which disciples are sent out to various towns. In between the two groups that are sent out we find a series of events which seem to alternate between two key questions. In the very middle of the set of passages under examination we also see the story of the Transfiguration. The Transfiguration is the key event, prior to the resurrection revealing Jesus as God's son. The hidden hand of the author of Luke, functioning as an editor with a purpose, seems to have placed these stories in this sequence for a reason.

We shouldn't underestimate the importance of the balance seen in the stories in this section. A focus on an event relating to the identity of Jesus leads to a story or discussion regarding discipleship. Conversely, after a pericope (or story about discipleship), the author reveals something more about the character of Jesus. There were two implied questions with the first being "Who is this Jesus?" The related question focused on those who would follow him and it was asking "What does it mean to follow him?" Those who are sent out must be committed, and their commitment must flow from a mutual understanding about the identity of Jesus as the Christ as well as the consequences of that faith.

One of the reasons this set of passages was so important to the author of Luke is that he used the term *apostles* in a striking way in the early part of this section. In the first verse of the ninth chapter it is said that the "twelve" were called together and sent out to preach and heal. When the twelve come back in 9:10, however, they are called "the apostles." This word "apostle," in its Greek roots, means "one who is sent." Luke tells us that, to earn this appellation, the disciples first had to be sent. The term "apostle" took on great importance in the life of the early Christian community and was, obviously, used very carefully by Luke.

Another significant clue to the overall text may be found in the sentence, "the apostles told Jesus all they had done." (Luke 9:10) What they told Jesus isn't stated, however, at that point. Could it be that some of the new things we hear about in the second missionary effort involving 70 others contain the insights of the disciples who went out the first time?

Look at the new additions to the missionary instructions that come in the 10th chapter:

1. A new number are sent out, namely 70.
2. They are sent ahead of him to the places he plans to visit.
3. He gives them a reason for going (a plentiful harvest).
4. He refers to a shortage of laborers.
5. He tells them they are like lambs in the midst of wolves.
6. The list of things to leave behind is different and longer.

In terms of door-to-door ministry, there is a phrase here which I have found most helpful, and which I especially appreciate. Jesus sends the 70 *to all the places he intends to visit himself.* The ministry of the 70, and by extension, our door-to-door ministry, is a kind of **pre-evangelism** in which we are merely preparing the way for Christ Jesus. A person making a faith commitment, after all, is saying "yes" to Jesus and *not* to the person who extended the invitation.

Rather than focus on all the small details involved with the story about sending out the 70 disciples, for the purposes of this study, we really need to pay attention to the command in Luke 10:7: "Remain in the same house, eating and drinking whatever they provide, for the laborer deserves to be paid. Do not move about from house to house." *That particular instruction seems to run totally counter to the spirit of the invitation ministry proposed in this book.* We're moving from one door to the next. Jesus told his disciples to find one house and to say there! How do we make sense of this command—to say nothing about all those who practice this ministry based on this very text?

In order to make sense of the discrepancy between Jesus' instructions and the actual practice of door-to-door ministry in our time, we need to remember exactly what Jesus told the disciples. There were to seek *one home*, a single house, *in a town* that would offer them sanctuary. If no such house is to be found, they must move on—in protest—to another town. (Luke 10:10–12) We need to ask, Why is it so important to find *a house* (singular) that gives them welcome? I think the answer is clear. Such a house is a **base for doing ministry in the larger context of the town where this house is located**. Having a home base means that it is possible to replicate the ministry of Jesus—a ministry, following his instructions, which would involve healing and preaching. In Luke 10:9 the command is to "Cure the sick who are there and say to them, 'The kingdom of God has come near to you.'"

The kind of door-to-door ministry encouraged in this book is most faithful to the spirit of Luke 10:1–9, because of **the importance of the local faith community** in the whole enterprise. *It's the base of our ministry!* We are inviting people who don't have a faith community to know they are welcome to attend the place that gives us nourishment in our faith journey. The presumption is that strangers who visit the church will encounter the healing and saving power of Christ in the sacraments and fellowship of the community. The same sacraments and the same fellowship provide the foundation for the missionary-work in the larger community. In the context of ministry, Christians find great personal strength, for example, in the weekly gathering for worship, and in the church I serve that means a weekly celebration of the Holy Eucharist. On one level we come into the Eucharistic fellowship with many personal needs, including the need to be forgiven and reminded of our acceptance through Christ. Beyond the personal and private aspects of spiritual nourishment in the Eucharist, there is a corporate and worldly context. At the end of each celebration, for example, there is a dismissal as we are sent back into a hurting world to serve and represent Christ. We are not only to find Christ present in the Eucharistic community, but we are to take Christ with us.

In my reading of the missionary mandate given to the 70,[5] Jesus was telling them that they could only exercise a healing and preaching ministry if they also had a community that gave them encouragement and support. Once they found such a supportive and welcoming community,

---

[5] Some manuscripts give the number as 72. Scholars disagree about which number was originally meant because the number 72 is a key reference to the 72 princes and languages of the world. Equal weight can be given to the number 70, which symbolically stands for the 70 elders of Israel, the 70 members of the Sanhedrin, or the 70 nations of the world.

they would be able to share fully in the ministry of Jesus. That ministry was not, however, to be based in the gathered community (the *ekklesia*[6]), but rather to be exercised beyond the community.[7] I think that we sometimes have lost sight of this truth. Too often the word *ministry* is what happens inside the gathered community of the faithful. In the spirit of Luke 10:1–9, I think we can see it is the reverse. Ministry happens when we have found a community, but that community is not the object of the ministry.

When I teach about the Biblical foundation for door-to-door ministry, I put it in the context of Luke 10:1–9 because this passage makes such a clear distinction between the function of the gathered community of Christ's friends and the focus for their ministry. We are gathered together so that we might be sent out to a world that needs the healing touch and word of Christ.

～

---

[6] Ekklesia is the Greek word often translated as "church," but our understanding of the word church is probably different from that found in many of the epistles in the New Testament. There is refers to a gathering of people in the sense of people being called out of something and then called together to be something different.

[7] The Greek word *ekklesia* isn't just a private gathering. It is a gathering that has always been understood as related to the larger community, and in existence for that larger community. In that sense, the church—the *ekklesia*—is still the church, even when it is sent out into the world.

Chapter 4

Conversational Evangelism

I hope it is clear by this point in the book that I am advocating a non-confrontational approach to evangelism. Initiating a conversation with a stranger must involve respect (and a strong listening component), while at the same time making an invitation. Sometimes the person to whom we are talking may be rooted in a religious view of life, but there's an equal probability that they're caught up in the secular world, and maybe even fearful of those with a religious perspective. Charles Taylor has noted that we live in a society "…in which for the first time in history a purely self-sufficient humanism [is]…a widely available option."[8] It is a world marked by disenchantment that has now become "…a universe ruled by causal laws, utterly unresponsive to human meanings."[9] One must thus conclude that many are best described, by the emphasis on their individuality, as "…the buffered self, which comes from living in a disenchanted world."[10]

We will have fewer and fewer conversations with people rooted in the stories of the Bible and the traditions of Judaism or Christianity. To

---

[8] Charles Taylor, *A Secular Age* (Cambridge MA: Harvard University Press, 2007) p. 18.

[9] Ibid. p. 280.

[10] Ibid. p. 300.

be sure, some parts of the population in America are still marked by deep religious sensibilities. But in many communities, that is part of the past, not current, history. George Hunter III, in his book *How to Reach Secular People,* saw this coming.

One of the major changes in the past 50–100 years is the way in which Christianity has lost its voice in affecting issues and events in the Western world. The erosion of influence is what Hunter calls "secularization." He defines this process as "...the withdrawal of whole areas of life, thought, and activity from the control or influence of the Church."[11]

What this means in terms of the lives of many people in our society is that their awareness of what happens within the world of the church is often marginal at best. Hunter suggests that the vast majority of secular people fall into three types, and only with the third type do we find some passing acquaintance with Christian thought and practice. The first group he calls "ignostics" because they simply don't know the language of Christians. The second group, called "notional Christians," may have some vague ideas about Christianity because they assume that this is a Christian culture. With the third group we have "nominal Christians" who may be occasionally active in a church, but who basically practice a kind of civil religion.

In the process of doing door-to-door ministry, the chances are that we will encounter all three types of people with minimal or non-existent religious roots. We are also going to meet increasing numbers of people who are attached to one of the growing number of non-Christian religions. Some of those belonging to these other faiths will be trying out that expression of religion as they seek to follow their yearning to discover God. We need to be sensitive to such pilgrim people because the invitation to know Christ, born out of curiosity and need, may lead them to the door of the church that we are sincerely trying to keep open.

---

[11] George Hunter III, *How to Reach Secular People.* Nashville, Abingdon Press, 1992, pp. 25–26.

One of the significant points that Hunter makes is that our age is starting to resemble the apostolic age that gave birth to Christianity. The four characteristics of that time were as follows:

1. The church faced a culture with no knowledge of the Gospel.
2. People tended to be hostile; the need was to "win friends and influence people."
3. There were other entrenched religions.
4. People needed to be invited to follow the way of Christ.

It is interesting to note that these are exactly the same issues we are facing today. I am convinced that it will be relational evangelism that will win the world for Christ. As we come to terms with the changing world, we need to accept the way the rules have changed. At the same time, the opportunity is as great as ever. I am constantly amazed by the opportunities we have whenever I go calling. The words of Jesus about having a plentiful harvest and a shortage of workers are as true today as they were when first spoken.

It isn't enough, however, just to recognize how the culture has become more secularized. It doesn't do any good, either, simply to lament the good old days when the culture seemed to support religious faith. If Hunter is correct in his assessment, as I believe he is, the times call not for retreat from the secular world, but for engagement.

Sadly, from my perspective a majority of leaders in our churches are stuck in their offices most of the time, possessed as it were with responsibilities for the existing church. We tend to remain enclosed in the structures of our Christian language and systems while we watch the world pass by. There are exceptions to this rule, however. One of the distinguishing marks of some of the great evangelists has been their willingness to get out of the stained-glass world and into the lives of those who make up the mainstream of their culture and society. Most-pastors will tell you that exegesis of the scripture text is essential to a good sermon. I add that we are called to exegete our culture as well and that was what characterized the great evangelists.

A case can be made that this ministry follows in the footsteps of John Wesley, the missionary clergy who planted churches among pioneer families as America grew. It's the spirit of church planting to reach people who are making a new life in a new community. Following the spirit of this work, evangelists like Robert Schuller and Rick Warren have done the kind of door-to-door ministry described in this book. Such pastors have made it a point to get to know the people whom they want to reach.

The method that Rick Warren used was to go door-to-door trying to find out what people would like to find in a church if they were going to look for one. After introducing himself and stating the fact that he was starting a new church, he would ask permission to ask five simple questions.[12] They were as follows:

1. Are you an active member of a nearby church?
2. What do you think is the greatest need in this area?
3. Why do you think that most people don't attend church?
4. If you were looking for a church in the area, what kinds of things would you look for?
5. What advice would you give me as the pastor of a new church? What, for instance, could I do for you?

The questions that Warren asked may not be appropriate in every situation, but the idea behind them is certainly transferable. In the process of going out to meet people on their own terms, we go to listen and learn. We certainly have something worthwhile to offer and there are opportunities to talk about our faith. In most of our encounter with strangers when we are inviting people to discover what life is Christ is all about, it is critical to remember that *our credibility will be based not on what we say, but on our willingness to be receptive to the needs and issues of others.*

I have found it increasingly effective to ask people questions similar to the kind suggested by Warren. I remember asking a man who didn't

---

[12] *Building Bridges: The Art and Practice of Evangelistic Calling.* Grand Rapids, MI: Church Development Resources, 1988, p. 32.

have a church, "What will you be looking for when you start visiting churches?" He replied, "I want to find a church that wants to be involved in the community, where the people care about what happens." His response gave me the permission to talk about the social action programs of our church. A little while later, I asked a woman a similar question. This time I said, "What are the criteria you use when you look for a church for your family?" She replied, "We want a church where the children are in Sunday School while we are in church. I also don't want it either too big or too small." After she told me this, I was able to explain how children at our church share in most, but not all, of our worship.

One of the verses of scripture that I carry with me as a guiding principle for this kind of calling is "Welcome one another, therefore, just as Christ has welcomed you, for the glory of God." (Romans 15:7) The nonjudgmental accepting spirit of Christ, grounded in Paul's ministry to both Jews and Gentiles, has to be in the forefront of our encounters with all people. The spirit of the door-to-door calling advocated in this book, moreover, is to practice a kind of invitational evangelism that begins by establishing relationships with secular people. We are talking with our neighbors and laying the foundation that will lead them to know the fullness of God's love. This invitation, however, can never be forced.

There are many ways in which we as Christians can express an invitation to a secular person, and the best methods for this evangelism will be rooted in the ordinary relationships of our lives. The spirit of listening and learning from others should guide Christians in all their relationships. We certainly have something worthwhile to offer, but we don't always have to be speaking about "our" programs or "our approach to ministry." Not talking is sometimes a virtue, and when you sense that the other person cannot hear what you might say, the best advice may be simply to offer a prayer from your heart, not your lips. This kind of silent prayer is one I have offered many times in the process of making various calls.

It must be understood that "door-to-door" ministry is an additional evangelistic ministry, and not a substitute ministry. Door-to-door ministry serves to introduce the church to many new people, and in a few situations it can be extremely effective. We can no longer assume, for example, that people get to know their neighbors. In this mobile culture of ours in which people live and work with such varied schedules, it is easily possible to live on a street where you might know only a few of your neighbors. Door-to-door ministry, nevertheless, must always take a back seat to the power of an invitational ministry based upon ongoing relationships in our families, through work, or within a circle of friends. The Institute for American Church Growth believes that "...70 to 90 percent of persons who join any church in America come through the influence of a friend, of a relative, or of an acquaintance."[13]

It isn't enough, however, just to know that relationships are the evangelistic key. We also need to encourage our own people, those who attend church, to invite people they know, those who are part of the secular culture, to come to church. The issue before most churches is how to encourage their members to make these invitations. I have found that door-to-door ministry helps encourage this kind of relational evangelism. So often, for example, I have found myself telling stories about my calling with the members of my church.

The reader may wonder why I as a pastor put so much emphasis on making calls as part of my ministry. Didn't I have enough other things to do? How did I find time to go door-to-door? Good questions. Part of the answer is that I learned this ministry while planting a new church and thus saw it as essential to that task. Certainly after ten years of growth in our church—with its 200+ households, and average attendance of over 300 people on Sundays—there was enough to keep me busy. I knew something else, however, about the power of my door-knocking. It was one of the keys to encouraging members of my church to have a positive attitude about their opportunities for inviting others to the church. We also had times when others in the church would join me for a specific blitz of door-knocking in a neighborhood we hadn't reached yet. *I wasn't sending them off to do something I wouldn't do.* Many times I also shared

---

13   Herb Miller. *How to Build a Magnetic Church.* Nashville: Abingdon Press, 1987, p. 32.

in my preaching some of the things I learned about our community and the gifts of stories that this ministry gave to me.

One of my favorite stories happened on a Saturday just before Christmas. As I approached the door or a particular house, I noticed lots of Christmas decorations, including a lighted star over the garage and plastic lighted candles by the door. I said to myself as I walked up to the door, "I'll bet they'll be either Lutheran or Roman Catholic. This looks like a religious house." After introducing myself and asking the man at the door if they belonged to a church, he replied, "Oh no. We're atheists." I had heard that before and usually responded with an invitation to visit if the person ever wants to see what we are like, but I didn't say that this time. In contrast to my usual reserve, I found myself saying to this man, "Well, you sure like Christmas." This was one of those times when, as soon as I had said the words, I wanted to pull them back. The man at the door didn't hesitate to respond, however. He said, "Oh, we love Christmas. Thanks for coming by." As I walked away from that call, I also found myself muttering. "They like Christmas. But it's really our holiday, not an atheist holiday." Ever since then, I've laughed many times about this encounter and have enjoyed sharing this story with others.

As a pastor I have always encouraged people to invite their friends to come to church. It was only in the act of planting a new church that I took the risks of doing it myself. Somehow I suddenly became more credible. A spirit of *relational evangelism* can start to pervade a congregation when the leadership practices what is preached. Door-to-door ministry can serve to encourage others to talk about their faith in their own circles of friendship and acquaintance. You will learn, further on in this book, there is a way to apply this principle in door-to-door ministry by introducing members of your church to their unchurched neighbors. See especially Topic #15 in our next chapter: Chapter 5, "Dos and Don'ts of Door-to-Door Ministry."

Inviting Guests and Not Visitors

When I first started going door-to-door I was inviting people *to visit* our church. At least I extended that invitation if I discovered that they had some interest or at least some questions to ask about our church. Then like so many pastors do on Sunday at the time of announcements I would extend a warm welcome to all <u>our visitors</u>. That's the term I was in the habit of using until I read that places like Disneyworld no longer welcomed visitors. *All who came were considered their guests!* To be sure they were paying guests, but the attitude of the staff and service people was that those who came were to be treated in a special way and that meant thinking of them as their guests.

Many a home sets aside one or two bedrooms and they are called "guest rooms." As I reflect on the guest rooms I've stayed in, I remember being treated as a member of the family. Usually the host will tell me to have anything I want to eat from the refrigerator if I get up in the night. If I'm going out and might come in late they'll give me a key to the house—often mine to keep for the duration of my stay. What we usually say to our guests is "Make yourself at home."

These insights about treating visitors as guests led to a revolution in my thinking.. I stopped welcoming visitors. Instead I would say something like this, "We welcome all our guests who are here today. We hope you'll feel at home with us." Amazingly this terminology started to take root in the life of our congregation and I think if affected the kind of welcome that was being extended to our first-time guests. I encourage you to look forward *to welcoming as guests to your church* those who've greeted you at their door. Consider how it sounds to welcome your guests using the invitation found in my suggested greeting for your guests!

WELCOME!

We welcome all who
are guests this morning.
Please know how
welcome you are.
You'll find the Guest
Center out on the Patio
and there are people
there to answer any
questions you might
have. Thank you for
your presence this
morning. There is a card
in the pew rack. Please
feel free to let us know
who are using that card.
You can make that your
offering this morning.

~

Chapter 5

The Dos and Don'ts of Door-to-Door Ministry

The purpose of this chapter is to address a number of different topics related to the *practical aspects of "door-to-door" ministry*. These are not presented in any particular order of priority. Some reading this book may find that my advice isn't always practical or helpful given your unique context for ministry. That's fully understandable. I encourage you to adapt this ministry to your particular environment, context, or culture.

1. What to wear.

My colleagues in the ordained ministry of the Episcopal Church are often surprised to discover that I believe in "door-to-door" ministry, but they are often more astonished to discover that I carefully make decisions about when and where to wear my white clerical collar with its distinctive black shirt. In my normal church work, especially on Sundays, I'm comfortable in this more standard clerical dress, but *I don't wear this clerical garb while I am out calling.*

I have a couple of reasons for this particular dress code. Early into this new ministry, I began to think about asking laypeople to join me in making calls. If the clerical look was important to this ministry, then I would have to figure out a way to get them all ordained. That wasn't practical.

I also realized something else about looking like a priest. Whenever I stood at someone's door, I was a dead giveaway. They'd get to the door and surmise right away that I had a religious agenda.

Finally, I started to think about the fact that many unchurched people have good reasons to fear involvement with a religious community. Some people have been abused by various religious systems. As a result of one or more negative experiences, some people tend to lump all churches into the same pot. That may not be a fair assessment, but I suspect it happens quite often. Part of the good news of the Gospel is that there are churches that help people discover value and dignity in their lives. Our task is to help some of those more severely offended by negative experiences to rediscover the grace of God. If I stand in ordinary civilian clothes on someone's doorstep and help disarm them from a few of their negative thoughts about religion, then I believe I'm doing God's will.

Though I don't wear my clerical garb, neither do I wear my worst jeans. I usually dress in casual clothes. Often I would wear a Greek fisherman's hat, but that is just because it was usually found on top of my head. The point is to wear clothes that are decent, but which in a casual kind of way send a signal of openness and friendliness.

I believe a case can be made for members of a church wearing a distinctive logo shirt that is appropriate to the culture and our times. I have a friend, a new church pastor in Florida, who wears good-looking short-sleeved shirts that bear the name of his church and the town in which it is located. The name and location are neatly stitched on a breast pocket or on the collar. My pastor friend and members of his church could all make calls wearing their church logo shirt people—it could be another point of identity for their church!

2. Wear a nametag.

The nametag idea is so simple and basic. My nametag is the one I wear at church on Sunday mornings, which contains our church name and symbol. My name is printed in 24-point type and is quite easy to read from a few feet away.

A visible nametag serves as a kind of badge lending a certain amount of safety to this encounter. Those calling must always bear in mind the fear element on the part of the person who answers the door. This training book emphasizes that factor often because it is one of the barriers we must face in order to create the relationships that lead a person to the Christian community. People in the service industry and those in law enforcement also wear nametags that make them easily identifiable. We all know how much easier it is to greet someone if they are readily willing to identify themselves.

Another reason I wear the nametag is that I want the person who stands at the door to remember me and my church. A new prospect for the church will receive at least one follow-up visit, and a nametag helps them remember both my name and the name of the church. More than once, I've noticed someone standing at the door staring at my nametag. I know the nametag is important to wear. Actually, I require people representing our church to wear a nametag when they are engaged in this ministry.

3. Keeping records.

There are a number of important reasons for keeping careful records about the calls you have made. First and foremost is the need to be economical and practical with the time we have to do this ministry. It doesn't make any sense to call on people more than once if they already have a happy church home. This calling primarily seeks to establish relationships with people who don't have a church home. Since respect of other religious traditions is basic to the kind of invitation I am advocating it is important to note which homes claim an affiliation with a church. When going back to do follow-up calls on a street where calls have been made, the record book shows which homes have already been visited.

Every time I studied those records, I saw something about all of the homes already visited. If they belonged to a church, that information appeared in the records, for example. I used my own coding for the various denominations, religions, and churches in our community. An "RC-JN" was a Roman Catholic attending St. John Neumann Parish. And "RC-MM" attended the parish called Mary Mother of the Church. I use the following designations for each of the major religious groups in our community:

RC	Roman Catholic
M	Methodist
P	Presbyterian
B	Baptist
Evang	Different Evangelical churches
Free	Free Church
Cov	Covenant
AoG	Assembly of God
DNWC	Do not want church
HAVE	Have a church, but would not say which one
Ep	Episcopal
L	Lutheran
x	Left a brochure, no one was at home

When you start calling, you will need to come up with your own record-keeping system. You may not choose to record things at the level of detail that mattered to me, but you want your record book to guide you when you go back into a neighborhood. I didn't need to knock on some doors twice, while there were other houses I really wanted to visit again.

My particular coding system assigned prospects either a number "1" or "2." A number "1" was considered a likely prospect who expressed an interest in finding a church. Usually, the person identified with a "1" had said something indicating interest, sometimes with direct questions about our church or they shared something regarding their own spiritual journey and search. I found it helpful when making a follow-up call to have this kind of information recorded in the calling notebook.

Another reason to keep careful records is to know the composition of the community where you are serving. If you're in the religion business, which I was, it is important to know what traditions are represented and what the trends are within the community being served. It was interesting, for example, to have a local banker ask me when we were applying for the church's first building loan if I knew anything about the religious inclinations of people in our area. I gave the banker a long report based on information gathered from my calling. You may want to have the same kind of understanding of your community.

Good record keeping also allows you easy access to personal information about prospects when making follow-up calls. If someone said they wanted to have a Sunday School for the kids, I might stop by to tell them about a special program we were having. If someone else said they'd probably come for Easter, that was another reason to stop by if I found myself in that neighborhood a few weeks before Easter. Having that data at hand made it much easier to do a follow-up visit.

When it is time to send prospects information about the church, you can pull up their names on a computer very quickly. Keeping all this calling information in a usable format without the help of a database computer system would be a most time-consuming task. In our case, we entered all the information about new residents on the computer on a monthly basis and then updated the information as additional calls were made.

In my church we had a volunteer who came in once a week to keep the calling book current. The person who did this was someone found through our door-to-door ministry. While this person didn't see herself as a person able to make these calls, she was more than happy to assist us in this ministry by keeping our records up-to-date. She was pleased to sit in an office while I was happier out knocking on doors with other courageous souls from our church.

4. What is the best time for calling?

The answer to this question will vary somewhat from one community to another, but I discovered two primary times for the best calling in the area where I served. My calling either took place between 5:30 and 7:30 P.M. on a weekday evening[14] or from 11 to 5 on a Saturday afternoon. If I tried calling at any other time, there were fewer and fewer people at home. At the best of times, usually over the dinner hour, the maximum percentage of people home would be about 60%, and more often than not it was closer to 50%.

Choosing an early evening time meant it was likely I would interrupt someone who was making dinner or who was just sitting down to eat. As a caller, I always felt uncomfortable when this happened, but I knew I had to choose a time when more people were at home. When it was obvious that someone had gotten up from the table to answer the door, I apologized for the inconvenience *and immediately assured them* that I only wanted a couple seconds of their time. Such words often helped make it a pleasant exchange for both of us.

5. Acknowledging the interruption that takes place with each call.

One of the things that I emphasize in my training of callers for this ministry is that they will cause some kind of interruption when they arrive. There is no way to avoid this reality. All they can do is bear it in mind. Therefore, it is critical that callers start out with the intention of keeping these visits rather short. This includes second and even third— visits. As callers, we need to have our antennae turned outward. If we catch someone in the midst of a phone conversation, we can say, "Excuse me for coming just when you were on the phone...." Such an apology often disarms those who wonder who it is that is knocking at their door.

Eventually, you start to discover people who are genuinely interested in knowing more about your church, and they will start to ask questions.

---

[14] Please note that the time of year and the weather also entered into the picture. I never called when it was getting dark. Living in a northern climate meant that as we moved into October, every fall, my calling was restricted to Saturdays, as it usually was getting dark around 6 P.M in the late Fall.

They may even invite the caller in to stay for a while. My strong recommendation is *to not accept such an invitation* when this is your first call at this particular house. I have learned to be quite cautious in such situations. Both men and women doing this calling need to be extremely careful about stepping into the home of a complete stranger. More often than not, there is absolutely nothing to fear, but you should always be aware of the possibility.

Sometimes it isn't an invitation to step inside that occurs, but a long conversation starts to take place at the door. In either case, I advise the caller to try to make an appointment for another time. The script I suggest is something like this:

> "I'm glad for your interest in our church and appreciate your invitation to come in so I can tell you more. But let me ask if we can set another time for me to return. This is my best time to call at other homes in the neighborhood. What would be a good time for me to come back for a visit when we both have time?"

No one has ever insisted that I come in and talk after I have made an offer like this. And if they ever had tried to persuade me, I would be even more resistant to staying. This ministry is not about the first visit anyway.

6. Respect of other traditions.

I am sure there are some of my Christian brothers and sisters who will take issue with me on this next point, but it is important to my sense of Christian charity to be clear about the respect I believe we are called to have for others and their beliefs—or even their refusal to admit to having any faith. No matter what someone tells me is or is not their religious tradition, I never try to persuade them to change. Part of my reason for saying this is due to the spirit of economy suggested elsewhere in this book. Why take the energy and time to try to impose my belief system on someone when there are so many people who are more receptive to the invitation I am making?

Even more relevant to our mission, however, is *the goodwill* that we should be creating in the wider community through our public witness. If I fail to show respect for other traditions, I will miss the opportunity to demonstrate the charity and grace that is at the heart of the Christian story. I would rather see Christians err on the side of showing tolerance and love than on trying to force someone to change their religious faith.

This emphasis on respect for other traditions does not mean, however, that we ought not make a warm invitation. Many a time I've stood on the doorstep of a Buddhist and I've said as I left, "I respect your faith. But I do want you to know that you would always be welcome to visit our church." That is all we need to say. Of course, if they do want to know more about us, we should take the opportunity to talk with them. In that case, of course, it would be most advisable to come back for another visit.

7. How to talk to children.

Many times the person answering the door will be a child. I always try to respect their dignity and personhood. At the same time, I make a specific request to speak to the adult who is present in the house. After I say "Hello" to them, I then ask, "Could I also say Hi to your Mom or Dad?" Usually they will then call for one of their parents to come to the door.

While we need to engage children as real people in this calling, we must also remember we are new to them. Many children have rightfully been taught to be wary of strangers, and that is correct, given some of the realities of crime in our time. When I find children alone at home, therefore, I make it a point to not ask them any questions, and I certainly don't expect them to tell me about their church affiliation. We must not take advantage of the innocence of children in this ministry. If no adult can come to the door, I merely leave my church brochure and ask the child to pass it on to Mom or Dad. In those cases I note in my records that I simply left my brochure. I count the visit as if no one was home.

8. Getting the church brochure into their hands.

A brochure is an essential part of the calling process. It is a communications tool with information about the life and services of our church. The brochure is not only a tool that gives the caller credibility and identity, but a kind of gift as well, especially for someone who might be looking for a church.

The goal is simply to get the brochure into the hands of the person who comes to the door; it isn't to read it to them. In training sessions, I usually encourage callers to practice this part of the procedure. As the person at home comes to the door, the caller needs to hold the brochure in a ready and visible way, actually moving their hand with the brochure toward the door. The nonverbal signal is that the caller has some information to share. If this process is done well, the person inside will normally open the door and take the brochure.

When someone does not open the door and take the brochure, do not make an issue of it. Likewise, if someone hands the brochure back to you saying they don't wish to keep it, accept it graciously.

The key is to practice handing the brochure to the person at the door at the same time as the introduction is made, though the introduction need not refer to the brochure. There is a nonverbal understanding in our society about accepting literature from a stranger.

9. Sending the newsletter or other invitations to prospects.

One learning from this form of evangelism is that sometimes it takes a long time for a prospective member to make that first visit to the church. The process can require repeated home visits and chance encounters. For someone who has been identified as a prospect, church newsletters and media stories about the church can serve both as a reminder of, and an introduction to, the church.

I recommend sending the church newsletter to all prospects for a limited period of time—say, for a year. Our church's newsletter contained a note near the mailing label that explained that people discovered through our door-to-door ministry who had no church home would receive this newsletter for a year. The note also stated that anyone could have their name removed from our list by simply calling the church office. The reason this notice was placed on each newsletter was that I never asked prospects if they wanted to receive the newsletter. Not only was that too much to ask on an initial call, but I assumed that most would refuse that offer. Since it was a newsletter they had never seen, how could they give a knowledgeable answer to that question?

The newsletter of our church, moreover, was also carefully edited and written with our prospects in mind. The activities and news of the church were emphasized in the version of the newsletter that was sent to prospects. (Yes, we had two newsletters each month. The prospects only saw the "newsy" one. When we had schedules or calendars to send out, we did not send them to prospective members who would obviously have little interest in the internal mechanics of church life.)

Sending prospects the newsletter was actually, and not too surprisingly, a major help when doing follow-up calls. Several prospects asked me about some event in our church, and I would reply, "Oh, you must have read about that in our newsletter." Others thanked me for the newsletter. To be sure, there were a few people who wanted their name taken off the list—perhaps seven or eight out of thousands of households visited. At least one family made a specific request to stay on the list even though they didn't attend.

This prospect mailing list was also useful for special promotional information about Easter and Christmas services. At these times of the year, more unchurched people will visit a church, and it makes sense for them to visit a church where they have already established some connection.

10. Remembering the basics about communications.

Experts in communications theory tell us that more messages are sent and received nonverbally than through the spoken word. For this reason our appearance, posture, facial expression, and gestures all matter a great deal when we talk with someone. The earlier suggestions about how to dress, for example, relate to this concept. In addition, our faces can communicate friendliness and interest in the other person. I suggest to callers that, before the first word comes out of their mouths, they should have already greeted the person coming to the door with a smile. It is important, in fact, to stay alert at the door in order to make immediate eye contact and to tell that person, using nonverbal cues, that this is a friendly caller at the door.

Then there is the matter of social distance. This is an extremely sensitive matter, particularly when a man calls and a woman answers the door. In our society there is a justifiable fear of the stranger. When calling, we can do a few things to lessen that fear so that a meaningful exchange can take place. It certainly helps to wear a name badge declaring your identity and that of your church. In addition, the caller should consciously increase the social distance immediately upon starting the conversation. This means that taking a half step back after handing the brochure to the person answering the door reduces the tension. The added distance (not required among friends) is a helpful way to ease the unspoken uncertainty in the mind of the person standing at their door. As we ease their anxiety by this nonverbal action, there is a greater likelihood for a meaningful exchange. There are, of course, cultural differences in the "comfort zone" preferred by people, a reality that cultural anthropologists study. My best advice is that it is always better to start further apart on an initial visit.

What about gestures and what we do with our hands? Many men, for example, are in the habit of talking with one or both hands in their pockets. In this situation it is really best to keep both hands out, and then to be careful to limit gesturing. A kind of cautious reserve is wise when meeting a stranger.

Another consideration is the sense of smell. It is not wise to wear cologne or perfume that is easily distinguishable. To do so simply invites someone to remember your smell and not your invitation. Posture is another thing to bear in mind since a straight back conveys energy and enthusiasm, factors that happen to be at the heart of the message we wish to bring with our invitations.

The last and perhaps most important aspect of this encounter, in terms of nonverbal communications, concerns physical contact. While it is often true that people in our society greet each other with a handshake, it is not necessary when making the first call in this ministry. Part of the reason for this observation is that by handing the person your brochure, you have made an initial exchange, albeit without human touch. Given the prevalence of uncertainty about the intentions of a stranger at our door, it is best to minimize anxiety by avoiding touch. At the end of some conversations, though, the situation can be different. Sometimes, I have found the other person reaching out to shake my hand as a way to express their friendship and gratitude for the call. In that situation it is appropriate to respond.

11. Maybe you shouldn't go calling two by two except for one practical reason.

Many people grounded in scripture like the idea of taking the words of Jesus to heart, and try to make these calls in the company of a friend. Some religious groups who take door-to-door ministry very seriously use the two-by-two method. The existence of this practice, in fact, is part of the reason that I recommend making these calls in a singular fashion. Two people standing together at the door of a stranger sends a nonverbal clue. The common perception of members of my church was that they knew right away these people are "out to convert them." I put that phrase in quotes because it is usually expressed as a negative when people tell stories about those who call at their house. I have tried to use a method that avoids confirming old fears and prejudices.

In teaching door-to-door ministry, I emphasize that "one-on-one" calling is usually more effective because it can be a more pleasant experience for the one who answers the door. The negative signals about "here they are again" just aren't there if you stand alone at the door, wearing a smile and with some ready identification that is visible. If done correctly, such a call can actually encourage an unchurched person to come to worship. The surprise to the person being visited is that there is no heavy-handed judgment being made. There is simply an invitation to visit.

It is possible, however, for two people to make such a visit without being perceived as "another set of religious callers on the doorstep." Sometimes, when introducing this ministry to someone, you may discover that they appreciate having both a coach and a friend go with them on their initial visits. I have trained many a caller this way. After all, sharing this experience with a friend and colleague can be a positive experience. Also, when a person is learning to make these calls, it is helpful to observe someone who has experience. The more experienced caller can offer helpful advice after a few calls have been made.

I suggest that when two people want to call together, one person stand down on the sidewalk (not on the front step), or at least they keep maybe at a distance of four or five feet away, while the one doing the calling stands at the door. I especially advise this method whenever women are involved in the calling. I am old-fashioned enough and also have enough social conscience to say that women should not be making these calls unaccompanied. There may be neighborhoods, though, where this isn't an issue.

12. Observing the signs around us when standing at the door.

It is important to remember that this kind of calling is all about establishing relationships, or simply making new friends. We never know what can happen, but all our meaningful relationships involve some shared values and interests. Many of us know that some of our best friendships began in a simple way, often with a conversation about something happening at a particular moment. If you engage in door-to-door ministry, you will find yourself with many such moments of opportunity. Some of the best advice I can give you, therefore, is to be observant whenever you start to approach a door for the first time. Here are some questions to be asking yourself:

1. Are there children living here? Approximately what ages?
2. Any pets?
3. Any hobbies (gardening, crafts, piano, etc.)?
4. What do you smell? Brownies? Garlic? Something on the barbecue?
5. Do they seem to represent a particular ethnic tradition with the things they have and the way they decorate?
6. What kind of cars do they drive?
7. How do they spend their leisure time? Boats? Golf equipment? Bikes? (Hint: open garage doors tell you a lot.)
8. If they are new residents, their old license plates may tell you where they lived previously.
9. Do you see moving boxes around? If you do, they may have recently arrived.
10. What do you remember about the adults you met?

This list could go on and on. The point is to be a silent note-taker picking up on at least a few clues that will help you relate to this person. I remember, for example, calling at the home of a man who had a blackboard hanging in his garage. On the blackboard he had written the names of his two cars and dates of the last oil change. Our conversation went something like this:

George:	Hi, I'm George Martin from Ss. Martha and Mary Episcopal Church here in town. I'm out letting people know about our church. I wanted to ask if you have a church you attend.
Man:	Not really. But I think my wife wants to go somewhere.
George:	Here's a brochure on our church. We'd welcome you all to check out the church. Have you been looking at various churches?
Man:	I haven't, but my wife has.

George:	Well, give her this brochure, if you will. By the way, before I go, I must tell you I really like something I saw in your garage as I walked up the driveway. I saw your blackboard with the dates of the last oil change. That's a great idea.
Man:	Thanks. I did that about 20 years ago. And I move that blackboard with me every time we move.
George:	I think I'll put up a blackboard in my garage. I can never remember when I did the last oil change.
Man:	That was always my problem. It sure helps to have that up there.
George:	Well, thanks for the idea.

This exchange was possible because I had seen something that was important in this man's life, and being the one in our house responsible for oil changes, I found it helpful since it was something that mattered to me as well. By noticing his blackboard, I connected to his creativity and ingenuity.

13. Follow the UPS method when ringing the doorbell.

I'm not sure who should get credit for this method, but every time I used to receive a package through United Parcel Service, the delivery person did two things: rang the doorbell, and knocked at the front door. The two actions combined were an important part of their methodology in getting packages delivered in the most efficient way possible. [Note: I'm not sure if UPS still has this as a policy for their deliveries, but I can assure the reader that this method is still highly advisable.]

The UPS people didn't want to waste time waiting at the door if the doorbell didn't work. I discovered that, even when the doorbell did work, the addition of the door knock told the person at home that someone different was at the door. At least, the person standing there is not likely the little kid who rang the doorbell several times already that morning.

14. How to ask for a person's name.

Perhaps one of the hardest things about this kind of calling is asking for the person's name when the call has been completed. I had a kind of cardinal rule about this matter: I only asked for someone's name if they had shown, by their questions, any level of interest in our church. Only if I thought they had some interest in learning about the church did I conclude my brief visit by asking to know their name.

Here is a sample exchange in which I would ask for the name of a prospect.

George:	Good afternoon! I'm George Martin, and I'm from the Episcopal church here in town. I'm letting folks know about our new church, and wondered if you have a church home.
Woman:	Well, not yet. We're rather new here.
George:	Any idea what kind of church you'll be looking for?
Woman:	Oh, not really. We're quite open. Except it had better have a good nursery.
George:	The nursery we have. It's a key part of our Sunday morning ministry. You're certainly welcome to come and visit. This brochure tells you more.
Woman:	Thank you. I'll look it over. But you'll have to excuse me. I'm getting dinner ready.
George:	Certainly, I never stay when making these calls. But one more thing—I know I told you I'm George Martin. Your name is?
Woman:	Oh, I'm sorry. I'm Mary Smith.
George:	I'll try to remember your name, Mary. Thanks for saying "hello."
Woman:	And thanks for stopping by.

I admit that asking for someone's name, as shown in this example, seems a little bold. The sample conversation is actually what usually happened. Rarely was my question, "And your name is?" considered rude. It's a normal part of many conversations we have.

At times someone would decline to give their name. And the answer to that? "That's no problem. Thanks for letting me give you that information." Offer a smile and take a step back. There's another door waiting for you.

If you get the person's name, be sure to write it down as you walk away. Back at our church office, those names were entered into the church's database for prospective members, and they would receive some periodic mailings that used their real name. Using names on mailings to prospective member households is clearly more personal than labels that read "Resident" or "Occupant."

The most important reason to have the name of the person who showed some interest is that you have just started the relationship. Rarely, as I noted before, did a single visit to a home lead someone to come to our church. I learned that this ministry required some follow-up calls. As we all know, it makes a difference when someone actually remembers our name, when we meet them for the second time.

15. What to do when calling in the neighborhood of a parishioner.

Another very effective practice in door-to-door ministry is to call on all the neighbors of a regular member of your church. Since the purpose of this calling is to use friendship as the basis for an invitation to worship, neighbors already have a head start on that friendship process. Even if the neighbors do not know each other well, their proximity often gives them a starting point for a relationship.

Try to maximize the potential of reaching unchurched people by involving some of your current members. I once had an appointment with a member family to discuss baptizing their two children. Rather than simply show up on time, I arrived on their block an hour early and made calls on all their neighbors, asking my religious survey questions. When I then called at the home of the members, I told them about all the calls I had made, including the prospective family I found living right next-door. They knew their neighbors, but they didn't know anything about their religious life, or lack of one. What ultimately mattered was that their neighbors were interested in the same kind of church.

Encourage other members of the church to make the acquaintance of those in their area who don't have a church home. Even when you make the initial contact, it makes sense to have neighboring members do the follow-up. I remember that at one point, I gave one of my member families a list of three households on their block who were looking for a church home. I encouraged them to talk with their neighbors about our church and said, "And you can tell them that it was your pastor who knocked at their doors, and that he asked you to answer their questions with the real truth about the church."

16. Training people to do door-to-door calling.

While this book serves as a comprehensive training manual, it wasn't intended as mandatory reading for the average person in your church who might volunteer to make some calls. This particular chapter covers most of the basics in actually making calls. I suggest that this chapter has important information to share with those going out on behalf of your church.

The Importance of a Training Event
You will help allay a great deal of fear and misunderstanding if you hold at least one training event prior to sending anyone out from your church to do door-to-door ministry. Everyone going out on behalf of your congregation is your congregation's visible representative every time a doorbell is rung—in the same way that the voice of a person who is paid an hourly wage and answers the phone at a major corporation represents not just the chief executive officer, but also every other employee and all the stockholders. Your training event is a kind of quality control effort that is metaphorically meant to put your best foot forward.

Designing the Training Event

You cannot overestimate the importance of addressing the normal fears that people bring to this kind of ministry. Focus on the way the elements of this approach reduce anxiety from the caller's point of view, as well as greatly improving the experience for whoever answers at the door. It is critical that you are sending out people who understand that in nearly all cases the person receiving you at the door is most likely going to thank you for coming. Each caller, moreover, needs to understand how this ministry increases the goodwill that resides in the larger community in terms of the knowledge that people will have about your church. The things that make this work are the simple things like wearing a nametag, offering a smile, and not intending to stay for a long conversation. You may even start off with some highly introverted people, who are, understandably reluctant at first, but who will offer to do this over and over, knowing just how positive this ministry truly is. Remember to emphasize that we are simply inviting people to come and see, and that we have no expectations of convincing or persuading anyone about any matter of faith.

I suggest that you design the training event to include the following:

A) The basic premises of invitational evangelism.
B) A few of the Biblical basics, particularly that this is a kind of pre-evangelism, going to the places where Jesus himself intends to go.
C) The key elements that reduce tension for all concerned—most of what is in this chapter.
D) Scripted role-play as found in this book. (See Chapter 7.)

The scripts in the workbook were created after I had some difficult training sessions, in which we had open-ended role-play. Every time I'd ask someone to play the role of someone at home, I discovered they were often playing the role of being an angry atheist, or someone who's just had the worst day of their life, and this call was the proverbial "straw that broke the camel's back." People, as it were, tended to project their worst fears onto this kind of enterprise. The role-plays were often funny to observe, but they weren't helpful from a training perspective, because they weren't true to what would actually be experienced.

The reality is that, in nearly every instance in my vast experience, a pleasant civilized exchange of information was what took place with nearly every call that was made. Time and again, in fact, people thanked me for having stopped at their house. The negative impression many people have about this kind of calling simply isn't justified in the actual expression of this ministry.

An Extra Idea: When you simply can't call on people because of where they live!

Inviting the Pastor to Your Next Party

This isn't a title of a joke. I'm serious about this idea as a method for reaching people who live in apartments or gated communities. Many congregations have members who live in those places. Look at your parish list and identify those who just might be willing to host a party that will include some of their neighbors. It might be a New Year's Eve party, or maybe a Super Bowl party. Maybe they host a summer barbeque. The occasion doesn't matter.

Make sure your church member understands how this party gives them a chance to let others know about the church they love, but they don't need to knock on any doors. And the pastor won't knock on those doors, either. All that happens is that one of the invited guests is your pastor. Maybe a couple of others also attend the same church. Following the guidelines suggested here your goal is simply to make new friends, and be ready to listen to their questions and stories.

You should warn the person hosting the party that the most likely response they'll hear after hosting the party is "I met your pastor at the party, and I really didn't learn much about your church. She listened to me a lot, I guess. Can you tell me more about your church? What's it like?"

13. Please note that the time of year and the weather also entered into the picture. I never called when it was starting to get dark and certainly never at night. Living in a Northern climate meant that as we moved into October, every Fall, my calling was restricted to Saturdays, as it usually would start to become dark around 6pm in the late Fall.

Chapter 6

Door Hangers: A Ministry Tool with

Great Potential

About ten years into the history of the church I started, I received a phone call from a man who simply said his name was "Ken." He asked if I had time to answer a question. He was wondering if we did weddings at our church for people who didn't belong. I answered that I was willing to talk to anyone about performing a wedding. We had some rules to follow, but we were quite open to working with all kinds of people to help them get married. "What is your situation?" I asked. He told me that he was divorced and would be marrying someone who wasn't allowed by her church to marry someone who was divorced. I explained that we help people who were divorced get married, even though we also wanted to affirm the sanctity of marriage. I made arrangements to meet them, and that's when he told me that his name was Ken and that her name was Kathy. Just before Ken hung up, he mentioned one more thing: "Oh, by the way," he said, "you can stop leaving those damned door hangers about your church at our door."

I looked back in my records. We had started leaving brochures and door hangers at his house six years previously. Until he called, we had never talked. He'd never been home. Somehow, though, those door hangers had been planting the seeds that led to Ken's phone call. Years later, not only are they still married, but we keep up with each other through the mutual exchange of Christmas letters. They had joined the church I was serving, and though they moved a few years later they continue as faithful members of a church.

Why Door Hangers Can Be So Important to Your Evangelism

As I introduce you to the idea of creating door hangers, please note that I am assuming this is a ministry that involves numerous attempts to make your presence known in a particular geographic area. I am talking about a process of creating at least four or five door hangers each and every year (maybe more) and finding a way to distribute them. In this chapter I'll be talking about two separate parts of this process: what needs to be on the door hangers, and the process of distribution.

I presume in talking about door hangers that you'll use them in one of two ways:

A. **The door hanger is the tool in the hand of a caller who is doing door-to-door ministry seeking conversations.** This method, when seeking conversations along the lines of what I've already discussed, doesn't reach great numbers of people on a particular day of calling, but it does unearth some definite prospects for the church. Most of this workbook has been written affirming this method as the one with the greatest potential.

or

B. **Let's get this information out to hundreds of houses all at once—Blitzing the Neighborhood!** The door hanger is, thus, part of an effort to distribute information to a great number of homes in designated neighborhoods. This method does not preclude conversations, but the intent is to place the information in the *largest number of homes possible in a specific span of time.* The law of large numbers, as it is used in the world of marketing, presumes that a few will always be reached with the intended message when you distribute a message that also misses the mark with many people. This chapter discusses the use of **a mass distribution of door hangers** using a sufficient number of volunteers to reach many homes on a single occasion.

What I hope to convey is that, once your church decides to use door hangers as one of the cornerstones for its evangelistic ministry, it is going to be taking some giant steps forward in terms of reaching people, especially if you can envision multiple opportunities for using this method. **Using door hangers is all about repeating your message**, establishing a look and feel for your church, and demonstrating by *your successive attempts* that you really are in the business of welcoming people. Over time your message will begin to penetrate the consciousness of more and more people in the immediate vicinity, who, at the very least, are going to have a basic knowledge about your church. More than likely—if you use humor, and present your material in a lively and interesting manner—you will have planted the seeds that lead more and more people to have a positive impression of your church.

As you begin to think about creating your first door hanger, remember this: You don't need to sell the entire farm at once! No single piece of literature has to tell the whole story (as if that were even possible!). Your church needs to plan on presenting a series of door hangers, and you can take your time to spread out your messages. Ideally, the succession of messages will present a coherent picture. Once you establish such a plan, you will find that you can focus on various unique aspects of particular ministries and programs that the church offers. You need to look ahead at least 12 months and plan for specific times when a guest would be most welcome, and then emphasize what you have to offer that is most inviting.

Looking at a Plan for Door Hangers throughout the Year

Overview:

September/October
Fall education program
Blessing of pets
A fall festival event
Halloween
November/December
Advent/Christmas programs
Music concerts
Nativity program
January/February/March
Lent programs
Mardi Gras/Shrove Tuesday
Winter festival
April/May
Holy Week and Easter
Spring events
Garden planting
June/July/August
Summer education/Youth/Service events
Camp
Summer concerts

The average church—even a very small one—can probably find enough that is happening inside their church to put together a door hanger for one or more of the seasonal opportunities listed above. A more program-oriented church will also want to consider using door hangers for some or all of the following events and ministries:

Blessing of the animals
Halloween parties
Thanksgiving services

Music series and concerts
Special classes or speakers at church
Special service projects
Rummage sale or similar fund-raising event
Special annual events or celebrations
Retreats, quiet days, pilgrimages
Dedication of a building
Welcoming a new staff member to the ministry team
Visit of the Bishop or your District Superintendent
Public event taking place at the church
Youth trip fund-raiser (Let folks know about the car wash and what it's for!)
Visiting scholar or missionary
Special days to recognize people (see below)
Book club (specify each new book)

This list could go on and on. I've made this list as long as it is to demonstrate the tremendous potential a church has for inviting others to a wide variety of opportunities. Using door hangers can serve as an extremely effective tool if your church sees itself as having a primary relationship with particular neighborhoods nearby. Some of the ideas in this list also relate to the concept of Event Evangelism, as discussed in much greater detail in Chapter 8 of this book.

Putting Together an Effective Door Hanger

The basic size for most door hangers is 4.25 inches by 11 inches. Because some of the space involves a cut-out notch for actually hanging the piece on a doorknob, the available space for printing is somewhat less than the exterior dimensions. It may seem that you don't have enough space for sharing the news about some ministry or program, but you actually have quite a bit of space. (One thing to remember is that you will be creating multiple door hangers for different events.)

It is possible to purchase door-hanger blanks that can be run off on your own copier, thus saving printing costs. You may also use the services of a more professional printing service that can print thousands of door hangers, and which may use color, or be on a glossy card stock. The choices are endless.

The Web-site Connection

It is critical that you see your door hanger as leading people to discover your Web site or your Facebook connection. Once you realize the way these technologies relate, you are given the freedom to create a less wordy and more visually appealing door hanger, since many of the details about your particular event or occasion are explained in fuller detail through your Web site.

I recommend that the following components be found in every door hanger:

1. Some kind of head-turning ad or message! (Humor is great!)
2. A map showing the church's location and service times.
3. A bullet list of the key benefits offered at this time.
4. A short letter, preferably from the pastor, with a call to action in it for the event or occasion.

At the end of this chapter you will find help in creating a bullet list and writing the all-important letter. (See "What's a Bullet List?" and "Letter from the Choir Director".) I am recommending, of course, that your church create a number of different door hangers. They don't all need to contain a letter from the pastor, of course, since there may be others who can write the appropriate letter. The important thing is that you want to make the letters as personal as possible, conveying to the prospective member that there are real people at that church. That helps start the friendship process.

Your door hangers also need a kind of consistent look to them. They don't need to look expensive or be printed on glossy paper. Simply try to develop a look that you like that serves as a kind a branding for the sprit of the church.

Presuming that Door Hangers Are Affordable

Until now I haven't mentioned that door hangers are a really afford-able way to reach people. Most readers probably assumed this. They are inexpensive because you are using a standard-sized paper and of-ten printing in just one or two colors. Most important of all, if you are delivering door hangers with help from members of your church, you are saving all kinds of money on postage. For some churches the cost-saving aspect of this method is its most important feature. I wouldn't suggest, however, that your enthusiasm for this method be based on this advantage.

What makes door hangers so effective is *that they are able to go al-most precisely to the very people you want to reach.* If your church market includes specific identifiable neighborhoods, your church actually has a great advantage over churches that draw their members from a wide geographic area. A neighborhood-specific strategy allows your church to focus its evangelistic energies, efforts, and resources in a specific tar-geted way.

A form of Guerilla Marketing

Please don't let the term "Guerilla Marketing" scare you. It's a direct marketing concept that addresses a specific concern that many have of the advertising world. How can an advertiser have the assurance that they can actually deliver a message *to the very people they want most to reach.*? The concept of *guerilla marketing* is precisely about deliver-ing a message to specific individuals. This concept applies to putting door-knockers on the doors in the neighborhoods that your church spe-cifically serves. You will be leaving a strong positive message about your church at a particular cluster of homes within some easy walking or driving distance of the church. To be sure, you'll be leaving the message with some people who already have a church home and others who sim-ply aren't interested in ever attending church. That shouldn't matter to you. Even reaching these people is not a form of failure, as you want two things from everyone, even if they never attend. You want them to, first, be aware of the church, and, second, you at least want them to have some positive feelings toward your church and its attempts at ministry. If you can achieve this goal with most of those who receive a door hanger, you have accomplished a great deal. At the very least you have laid the foundation for the door hanger that will be distributed next.

The Community in Action: Distributing the Door Hangers

I can't think of a better way to engage more people in a positive experience of evangelism, than inviting them to pass out information about your church. You will need to create a level of enthusiasm and support for this ministry within the church on the first few occasions when you use this method. It is very likely that, eventually, the volunteers in this ministry will take on more responsibility for this ministry. It may be that recruiting new volunteers becomes something rather automatic and common in the life of the church. It probably will be harder the first time you do it, of course.

Meeting Their Fears Head-On. You can probably imagine what makes most people afraid about going out to deliver door hangers. "Will I have to talk to anyone? What would I say?" Such comments will often involve a touch of humor, but for some, the feeling behind the statement can be true fear. It will be important to assuage this anxiety right from the beginning of the process. It would be misleading to say that you'll never have to talk to someone. In your training, therefore, you may want to tell your volunteers delivering the door hangers, "Chances are someone will see you coming to their door, and out of curiosity will want to know who you are and what you are representing."

It is important, therefore, to train the people ready to assist with a door-hanger blitz. Every one who heads out, younger or older, is representing your church. Let them go out ready to distribute a great deal of information to a maximum number of homes in a short time. Let them understand how important this is to the future of your church, and the great positive influence this single effort at ministry may be having.

Make an Event out of the Delivery of Door Hangers

I recommend that you do all you can to make your door-hanger volunteers feel needed and supported for this ministry. If they are delivering these on a Saturday morning, for example, they should find everything waiting for them when they come to the church to get their assignments. Before the distribution, you will probably want to gather everyone for a half-hour or longer, so that you can review what's going to happen. When doing this for the first time or with folks who have never done this before, you may need to spend more time before people are sent out.

Have a nametag for all callers. This is a basic. Create nametags with your church's name clearly printed on them, and then put the full name of the caller on their nametag. They should wear that nametag on their upper right side in case they actually have one of those conversations I mentioned. Remind the callers that the nametag helps them look official and serves as a friendly way in which people in the community will meet them.

Offer food! If you are sending folks out in the morning, have coffee and donuts on hand. If calls are being made in the afternoon, have some kind of treats, iced-tea or soda available upon their return.

Prepare easy-to-read maps and assignments. It is really helpful for callers if someone has already mapped out the areas where the material will be delivered. Once this is done right, it can easily be repeated for future efforts. The initial task may seem daunting, but there are people in every church who can plan such an effort. Look for people who are good on details and who might have the time to do some counting and estimating about the number of homes in various neighborhoods.

Every caller should be given a map and clear instructions about the streets on which they will deliver the door hangers. Callers can be asked, of course, to work in teams. Two people will share the same street, but deliver door hangers on opposite sides of the street.

Callers should return to the church. Whoever is coordinating this effort needs to stay at the church to welcome people back. If it is a large calling effort, you may want to have two or three others (who have cars) stay as well. The use of cell phones can greatly assist this ministry. For example, someone might run out of door hangers, but have ten more homes to visit. A simple phone call back to the church can solve this problem, as the extra door hangers are brought to them. Cars may also be used to bring callers back to the church, and callers can use a cell phone when they have completed their route.

Celebrating the event: WE DID IT! Every time you do this ministry, you want to make those who did the calling feel really proud of what they did. Talk about the number of homes you reached. Encourage people to share any stories they may have about delivering the door hangers. Create an atmosphere back at the church to celebrate their accomplishment. If you've scheduled the next delivery, ask people to sign up to help with that, since there is a high likelihood that most who participated will be enthusiastic about what they have done. Make sure the names of those who participated appear in the church's newsletter and that information about the effort (how many homes were reached, for example) is also celebrated publicly in the church. All your attention to this part of the process will pay huge dividends as you continue with this ministry. I suggest sending a personal thank-you card to everyone who helped in this effort.

Plan to welcome many more guests at church! As your church takes this ministry seriously, you should expect to discover, especially over time, that there will be a new wave of guests following each door-hanger drop. The impact of this ministry is cumulative in nature as your church, and the programs it offers, become better known in the community. You may not actually find yourself running out of room on the first Sunday after you start this ministry. It may take weeks or even months for some people to respond. Many will not respond after the first piece of information has been delivered. Remember that this is about trust and familiarity. Because this is an affordable, repeatable evangelistic ministry, the true results emerge over time and not after a particular door hanger has been delivered. Having given such words of caution, nonetheless, I think that you should enter this ministry expecting to make a significant impact in your community. I wouldn't be surprised, for example, if you started with 1,000 homes, but then expanded your effort to include another 1,000 after discovering the impact that this tool can have.

You may also begin this ministry reaching a smaller number of homes (say, 500 or 1,000) because you're not sure if you can get the support within the church for delivering the door hangers. Eventually, as your members experience the excitement and meaning that comes from participating in this easy ministry, you will find it easier and easier to recruit more volunteers. Increased numbers of volunteers simply opens up the possibility of reaching a larger number of homes.

Words of Caution—Offering Guidelines to Your Callers

When sending out volunteers into neighborhoods on behalf of the church, make sure that you set out some standards and guidelines to protect them from any harm. You may want to adapt the following guidelines if they make sense in your setting.

1. Please wear the church's official nametag so that it is visible. Place on the right side of your coat or shirt.
2. Know that what you are doing is perfectly legal. Our constitution guarantees us the right to share information with our neighbors in this way. Be sure to check with local ordinances first regarding a possible need to publicize this event ahead of time or be registered with the city for this event.
3. It is good if people go out in pairs and keep an eye on each other. A rule of thumb for all should be "Stay in touch with your buddy." When covering a particular street, it works best if each person in a pair takes a different side of the street and then they catch up with each other at the corner.

4. When putting the door hanger on the door, it is best to use the most exterior door. Never open a screen door if the inside door is open into the house. DO NOT PLACE door hangers inside a mailbox. It's a violation of the law to place something in a mailbox unless you are an authorized carrier with the U.S. Post Office. (It can be OK to hang something on a mailbox, though, if there is a lower rack used for newspapers.) If there is really no easy place to hang the door hanger, don't worry about it. It's OK to skip that house. Remember: it's the law of large numbers.

5. When talking to someone who might come to the door, do not go inside. Stay outside where you are visible to your buddy.

6. If someone seems to have lots of questions about the church, it would be best to ask if someone from the church might call them later. Ask for their name and telephone number and assure them that someone will call them in a day or so.

7. If someone seems particularly interested in the church, it is good to ask for their name. Please bring their name and the address of where they live back to the church, so follow-up can be done. Try to remember what questions they were asking and anything about them that may assist those at the church doing the follow-up.

8. It's OK to avoid houses with mad dogs.

9. It's OK to walk away from a home if there is a sign that says "No solicitors" or something like that.

10. Do not take it personally if someone hands the door hanger back and tells you they aren't interested. Remember that Jesus told a parable about the Sower, and that only some of the seed fell on ground that was productive. We don't even have to judge the quality of the ground (how receptive people are). We're about sharing the story about our church.

11. Offer a prayer of blessing at every house where you leave the door hanger—a prayer that God will bless them and encourage them, and that they will know God's love.

In conclusion, understand that the door hanger ministry—assuredly a most affordable way for a church to engage in direct marketing— is simply a way to share some printed information with a larger number of people. Using the willing hands and legs of members of your church can save on the postage. It also allows for the timely delivery of your messages, and it can be a really positive experience for many people to help their church spread the word.

EXTRAS: HELP FOR YOUR DOOR HANGER DESIGN

I'm including a couple of suggested boxes that may help your Door Hanger more impact. The idea is to keep things simple and easy to read. You may make some key points about things your church offers, but it really helps to find a way to summarize those ideas, especially for people who do a quick-read of any kind of direct marketing piece. We get so many that come our way. What we don't realize is that there is what marketing experts call the "four second rule." The average person will take about four seconds to determine if there is anything in a particular direct mail piece that's worth reading. That's where a bullet list is helpful, because it offers a quick summary of what's inside. The same principle applies to the addition of a P.S. on a letter. That short sentence may be read first, and if it's a call to action, there's a chance the letter will actually get read.

What's a Bullet List?

- A series of ideas
- A quick summary
- Where the eye may go first
- A place to repeat what's important

A bullet list is a tool for a direct-marketing piece that has been proved to be an effective component of a brochure. It's not where you start to offer new ideas but it does create interest in your new ideas! It's a place that points back to the wordier parts of your piece. And if someone reads the longer part first, the bullet list re-affirms the important things you've already explained. The bullet list is like a word-based laser pointing tool!

Why a SHORT Letter Is Helpful!

You might be skeptical about the value of letter in a simple brochure or on a door-hanger. Many of us will declare, "Oh I never read those letters. That's just advertising." Many times we don't. That's absolutely true. But research has shown the power of a persuasive letter that bears the hallmark of some real person who is writing it. A longer letter can begin with a story or a personal example that can be the start of a kind of conversation. Even a short letter, such as I've offered here as an example, makes a clear offer and it answers all the key questions: what, when, where and why? It's the P.S. that summarizes all of the key ideas. Even though my suggested P.S. doesn't use a single sentence, notice how short the sentences are. When writing your brochure try to avoid long compounded sentences. Use strong verbs whenever possible..

Sample Letter
From the Choir Director
On a Door Hanger

Joy to the World

Trinity Church at 4pm Dec. 22nd

Dear Neighbors,
The Spirit of Christmas will be heard in song on Sunday, Dec. 22nd, at Trinity Church. It's a concert that children of ALL AGES can enjoy. Just an hour long it will conclude with a gift of carols you can take home with you. We'll include a free guide that offers ideas for keeping Christ in your Christmas.

Merry Christmas
Sally Jones
(Music Director, Trinity Church)

P.S. Come on Sunday to enjoy the music and receive a gift of music. (There's no collection—it's our gift to you!)
Come at four. Leave at five with your Gift of Carols!

Chapter 7

Door-to-Door Scripts

The purpose of this chapter is to give prospective callers some idea about various exchanges that are likely to take place when they are out calling. Earlier, I mentioned using open-ended role-plays when helping to train people for this ministry when I was first getting started and inviting others to participate. I would ask for a couple of volunteers and then have one of them pretend to call on the other at home. Often, these role-playing situations led to lots of laughter, but rarely did they reflect the true nature of this ministry.

Many of us have had people come to our door who clearly had an agenda to sell us some product or to convince us to believe something, and on occasion such people are persistent and leave only reluctantly. Seeing a stranger at the door sometimes leads us to fear that this is going to be a difficult conversation and may take up time that we don't have to spare. As you have probably already discovered, the method advocated in this approach is quite the opposite of what people expect. It is so important to remember that a great many people you meet, when you follow the guidelines in this book, will actually be thanking you for coming to their door. Consequently, it doesn't help to do role-playing that emphasizes our worst fears.

The scripts in this chapter offer people realistic scenarios, based upon the experience of the author, who has made thousands of calls. *Not once have I ever had a door slammed in my face,* and on only a few occasions was a person rather rude or abrupt with me. I don't offer a single example of a difficult call because I really have had so few. It is important to remember, as well, that this calling is all about looking for someone who is potentially interested in finding a faith community. When I find people who clearly aren't interested in joining a church, I make a note of this fact, say a quiet prayer for them, and then move on. I do not make follow-up visits on those who have told me either implicitly or explicitly that they aren't interested in the church.

When conducting a training event, it is advisable to print out these scripts and give a copy to each person who is willing to enter into the role-play. [*NOTE to the Reader*: Purchasing this book means that the reader has permission to copy the scripts in this chapter, as well as the guidelines found elsewhere to help in the training of door-to-door callers.] If it is a small group of, say, six to ten who are being trained, everyone can participate in one of these scripts. Someone should be the director who sets the stage with an imaginary door, giving one person the role of "caller" and the other role as that of someone at home.

After each role-play, ask the actors how it felt. Also, invite those watching to make comments. Sometimes it's important to ask the two actors to do the script again, perhaps reversing the roles and on the second take, allowing them (if so inclined) to improvise. Just remind them not to project their worst fears onto this hypothetical encounter.

1. A call when someone already attends another church

Most of the calling I have done has been in a part of the country where there is a high degree of church affiliation. More often than not, consequently, I was calling on people who had a church home. The following script was the one that I experienced many times.

Caller	Good afternoon. I'm "Joe Faith" with St. With-it Church. I'm out letting people know about our church and was wondering if you have a church that you attend?
Man at door	Yes, we do.
Caller	That's great. Which one is it?
Man at door	It's the Roman Catholic church, St. Bud's.
Caller	I know your pastor, Fr. Lite; he's wonderful. I'm not going to ask you to switch. We just invite those who don't have a church home. Thanks for your time. Have a great day.

Because I make it a point to leave a brochure on our church at every home, this person also received some literature on our church. Even though they are not a prospective member household, they are now more aware of our church. They have received a friendly call, and they did not experience any coercion. Chances are they have a more favorable impression of our church as a result of the call.

2. Finding a prospect

The following script shows what happens when a prospect is found. It is important to remember that a key concept of this evangelistic work is that we are trying to build a relationship with a secular person. As I emphasized earlier, these relationships emerge over time through different kinds of follow-up calls. Even if someone is really interested in the church on the first call, I have made it a point to keep the call relatively brief. The following script shows how I can obtain all the essential information and not overstay my welcome.

Caller	Good afternoon. I'm "Joe Faith" with St. With-it Church. I'm out calling, letting people know about our

	church, and was wondering if you have a church that you attend?
Mary	Well, not yet.
Caller	What do you hope to find in a church?
Mary	We have kids. They need a church.
Caller	I understand. We have Sunday School and it's a place where kids know they matter.
Mary	When we get a free Sunday, we'll keep you in mind.
Caller	Thank you. I'm George Martin and, if you don't mind, what's your name?
Mary	It's Mary.
Caller	OK. Mary. And ah…your last name?
Mary	It's Smith.
Caller	I can remember that. And you all feel free to visit. Thanks for your time. Have a great day.

One possible reaction to this particular script is, "But could you say more about your church?" My answer to this question is, "Yes! But I need to respect the fact that I have interrupted Mary and, while I understand the desire to say more, I will come back and say hello on another day." It's critical that we understand in our role-play that this is an invitational form of evangelism, grounded in the concept of making friends. We are not selling anything but are simply offering an invitation to visit.

3. A call when someone is simply not interested

As I suggested earlier, I have made very few calls during which I was treated in a rude manner. There have been times, however, when I have encountered coolness or disinterest. My response is always one of respect. As a representative of Christ and the church, my responsibility isn't to be persuasive, but only to offer an invitation. I've done that by coming to their door and handing them the brochure with a smile. The following script is an example of such a call.

Caller	Good afternoon. I'm "Joe Faith" with St. With-it Church. I'm out letting people know about our church and was wondering if you have a church that you attend?
Woman at door	No, not at all.
Caller	Well, I'm just trying to open the door to our church if you're looking around.
Woman at door	I'm not. I'm not interested in going to church at all.
Caller	I won't take up any more of your time. But if you ever decide to visit, please know that we'd welcome you. I hope you have a great day.

Because the method I follow involves handing the brochure to everyone I meet, such a person is left with a piece of literature about the church. I can certainly pray for this person and her family as I walk away. I also remind myself that it may take a neighbor, a friend, or a co-worker to extend the invitation. Door-to-door ministry doesn't take place in an evangelistic vacuum. It is just one ministry among many taking place in the life of a Christian community.

4. Finding someone with lots of interest

There are some occasions when a person at the door shows lots of interest in finding a church. The following script is an example of such a call.

Caller	Good afternoon. I'm "Joe Faith" with St. With-it Church. I'm out letting people know about our church and was wondering if you have a church that you attend?
Virginia	Not yet. But we've been visiting some since we moved here a few weeks ago.
Caller	You must have moved here from Virginia. I saw your license plate.

Virginia	That's right. We were in the northern part, quite near Washington DC. We attended a Presbyterian church—well, not very often. It was a rather cold church and we never felt they offered much for the children. Do you have a good Sunday School program?
Caller	We certainly do. Actually, there are two Sunday School times since we have two services. We share worship as well with the children. They know they are part of the church.
Virginia	Your church looks interesting. I have a lot of questions for you. Could you come in for a cup of coffee?
Caller	That would be great, but I wonder if I could make an appointment with you. This is the best time of day for me to call like this. It's going to be dark in an hour, and I'd be glad to come back later in the week.
Virginia	That would be fine. What about tomorrow evening around 7?
Caller	OK. That'll work. By the way, what is your name?
Virginia	Oh, I'm Virginia Churchshopper.
Caller	Thanks for your friendly welcome, Virginia. I'll look forward to coming back tomorrow night. Oh, one more thing. Do you have a DVD player? (She nods yes.) I'll bring an 8-minute video about our church when I come back. It's on a DVD we made.

There are a couple of things to notice about this call. The caller in this script doesn't try to close the deal, as it were. Once again, this kind of evangelism involves creating a relationship. It is so much better to let the relationship build through a series of encounters.

Another thing about this call is the refusal of the caller to stay. Such calling always causes an interruption, even if the person wasn't doing anything but watching the clouds float by. If a person wants to talk more about the church, it is best to have an extended conversation take place on a scheduled and planned basis.

Chapter 8

Event Evangelism: Door-to-Door
Ministry in Reverse

One problem with regard to door-to-door ministry is that it can take a considerable amount of time. In an hour of calling, for example, a single caller might be able to knock on twenty to thirty different doors in a neighborhood where the houses are perhaps some distance from one another. You might find people home in half of those homes, and from those homes where you meet someone, you might discover one or two prospects. Having others from the church engaged in this calling certainly helps, because so many more homes are reached in that single hour. What if there were a way, however, to reach a great many people with a single event? What if that event led people to come to you? Or where you found them out of their homes attending some community event in which your church was participating? This chapter discusses the ways this can happen.

My term for this kind of ministry is *Event Evangelism*. The word *event* is to be understood in a number of different ways.

1. *The event may be a community event and your church finds a way to participate in that event.*

or

2. *An event can be some festival or program that your church creates that is an offering for people in your community.*

or

3. *An event can be a service project that helps people in your community. It's something you give away or do for others.*

A key church-growth leader is Ken Callahan, who has written *12 Keys to an Effective Church, Strategic Planning for Mission.* Callahan's premise is that churches ought to have at least 12 times in a year when they are doing something through the church that is highly invitational and where nonmembers are going to be most welcome to attend. Basically, he says once a month there should be what I call an event.

On his Web site there used to be a wonderful Callahan quote with regard to each invitational opportunity:

The *Twelve Keys* are possibilities of grace.
You are welcome to approach them with a spirit of grace...a theology
of grace.
They are keys. They open doors for the possibilities
with which God is blessing your congregation.
They are opportunities for you to develop a strong, healthy
congregation,
sharing richly and fully in the grace and mission of God.[15]

I love the positive and hopeful way in which Callahan phrases this approach to ministry. One thing I would add, however, is that we need to approach these events with the spirit of giving a gift, knowing that this will be a joyful gift to give. This chapter will offer a few ideas grounded in the belief that event evangelism is great fun. The list of ideas here isn't exhaustive. My purpose is simply to stimulate thinking about the many different

---

15   The most current web address to find out more about Ken Callahan resources is http://
www.missionleadersnetwork.com/about-kennon-l-callahan

ways in which your church can invite and welcome people to know who you are and to have a relationship with God if such might be lacking.

1. Events sponsored in your community

Like many churches, the one I started (where I learned to do door-to-door ministry) met in an elementary school in the earliest years. We had purchased a rather nice trailer for hauling our electric piano, our hymnals and worship books, and our church school supplies. We also properly placed our church name on both sides of the trailer and advertised our worship times since the trailer was parked in a driveway on a busy street during the week.

The church was in a community that loves to celebrate the Fourth of July with a parade, fireworks, and a barbecue in one of the parks. Like many a small-town Fourth of July parade, this one always included fire trucks from various volunteer fire departments, floats for various realtors, and local politicians riding in their convertibles and handing out buttons and stickers to the kids. Some groups threw candy out to the kids. The local high school marching band participated, as did all kinds of other community groups. The first year I watched this particular parade, however, I didn't see a single church represented. The thought came into my head, "Why don't we pull our trailer in this parade next year, and why don't we hand out something to the kids?"

The next year we were entered in the parade for what really was a very modest fee. One of our parishioners used his truck to pull our trailer and we also had imprinted some T-shirts with our church's new name and logo on them. We wanted our people to be properly identified. The church's name was Ss. Martha and Mary, and we affectionately referred to our church as the "M&M Church." We purchased a few thousand very small bags of M&Ms and stapled them to little invitations to the "M&M"

church. Our bags of M&Ms ran out before we reached the end of the parade route, but our spirits never flagged and our smiles lasted the whole
way. When it came time to evaluate our participation in this event, everyone was enthusiastic about doing it again the next year but with one difference—we wanted our own float. So it was that, year after year, the church
had a float and a presence in every Fourth of July parade. (Eventually, with
the help of one member of the church who collected antique John Deere
tractors, we had a most distinctive look pulling our float.)

I know of another church that connected to a riverfront festival in
their city. This was a church with a lovely front lawn right at the center of
the city square. They had never used that lawn, though for anything but
growing grass. The year of the River Festival, however, the front lawn was
covered with picnic tables, lawn chairs, and barbecue grills. They were
serving inexpensive hotdogs and hamburgers, selling pop and coffee, and
most important of all, giving away free water. On the plastic water bot-
tle the church's name was boldly printed, along with the phrase, "Guests
Expected!" There was also a paraphrase of Matthew 10:42, which read,
"Give a cool cup of water to someone who is thirsty…the smallest act of
giving or receiving makes you a true disciple." The same church found
other events as well and began to use their front lawn more often to welcome guests. Rather than renting the tents used for their food booths and
to cover the picnic tables, they even invested in their own tents.

The point of these two examples is simply to suggest that there probably are many things happening in our world to which we as Christians
can connect in a positive way. I happen to believe that our participation
in these events is one way in which we really can witness to the love of
God and our belief in God's grace. And in many ways, our actions will
speak louder than words.

2. Church-sponsored community events

One of the best examples of Event Evangelism is the Johnny
Appleseed Bash sponsored every fall by St. Stephen's Episcopal Church

in Edina, Minnesota. This is a one-day event held on a Saturday in the city park across the street from the church. It is publicized in the community as a festival especially designed for children and families. The event offers a wide range of games, pony rides, dunk tank, face painting, and pumpkin decorating. Tickets are sold for all the games and rides, and every child receives points whenever they do something that afternoon. The points are traded for prizes displayed on long tables under a beautiful tent.

There are musical groups performing on a portable stage throughout the afternoon. A teen choir (sent by a local church) may sing, perhaps followed by a Dixieland band. Sometimes there's a public show as an intermission between the bands. Hamburgers and hot dogs, along with cotton candy and ice cream, are sold. There are large signs posted in a couple of very visible places, explaining that **all of the money** raised at this event is for community outreach. The groups in the community that benefit are listed by name. There is a sign on the front steps of the church (across the street), which announces free tours of the church. Clearly, this is not evangelism that involves any sense of coercion; it is all about an invitation to have a good time with your children or grandchildren. The pastor of this church will tell you that every year he learns of new members who joined the church because of what they experienced at the Johnny Appleseed Bash.

Another church in Tennessee loves to celebrate St. Francis Day. On the church calendar, October 4 is the designated day. This church chooses the Saturday that is closest to it every year. They will offer a blessing of pets and animals, and this is the service that usually begins their festival day. I like the fact that they invite veterinarians and folks from the local zoo to come. Those who offer dog obedience schools can put their material out for people. The local police officer with a K-9 dog may be on hand demonstrating how the dog helps aid law enforcement. They may even offer awards for the best-dressed cat or dog. One way to understand what this church is doing is that it is putting its reputation on the line, and everyone has to leave feeling good about how this church loves creation.

St. Matthew's Parish and School in Pacific Palisades, California has a very large annual event with the name "The Town Faire" every May. The school's meadow, used by the school for soccer and football, is filled on this one day with various carnival rides and many booths with games for children of all ages. The children can earn credit (tickets) they use to purchase from the Faire's toy store. A tent in the middle of the grounds features a blue-grass band. There are food tents around. The large field house on the campus is filled with vendors selling goods alongside the church's thrift store which saves some of its best items for this event. All of the money raised goes for outreach. Parking is always a problem—indeed a very nice problem solved by using a shuttle service and some golf carts taking people from their cars to the Faire.

In July each year there's a Roman Catholic Church near downtown Minneapolis with an event that reaches thousands of young adults. It's called "The Basilica Rock Party." Over two nights a series of rock bands take turns entering those who have bought tickets to this event. They serve food and beer (also for purchase). The money raised has been used for the much needed renovations on their old historic church. More importantly if you peek in the door on an average Sunday morning you'll see that a larger than expected portion of the congregation are people in their 20s and 30s!

No matter what kind of event it is that your church will sponsor, you should make it clear that it is a church-sponsored event with a specific purpose. To be sure, you'll understand it as a form of evangelism, but the purpose must fit in with something everyone in the community can support.

On the day of the actual event, I would insist that the members of the church be properly identified, wearing nametags that indicate they belong to the church sponsoring this event. It may help to have specific T-shirts or hats on member participants. It is critical that the leadership of the church also be on hand and visible. Just as handing out a brochure is important in door-to-door ministry, it is important that there be some information about the church available at events as well. That way, people can pick up a copy if they're at all interested.

If the event is something that becomes an annual thing, like the St. Francis Day Festival is for that particular church, then I encourage the development of a mailing list of interested participants. It's the same concept discussed earlier about creating a prospect list through door-to-door ministry. One way to place people on the list is simply to ask if they would like to be notified of next year's event; and if they would, there is a card that they can fill out with their home address and maybe even their e-mail address. Another way to get e-mail addresses is to have a free drawing—say for a basket of apples, or free apple pie—and let people give you their e-mail addresses as they enter the raffle. Maybe you simply add a little checkbox on that raffle ticket by which they allow you to send them notification of next year's event.

These are examples of events incurring goodwill, and which can be held on a yearly basis. The churches referenced in the stories above have members who really do look forward to each of these events, in part because they are simple one-day or two-day events. To be sure, there is an investment of time and effort but not the kind that goes on for months at a time.

3. Servant Evangelism

"Servant Evangelism" is a term used by Steve Sjogren in his book, *101 Ways to Reach Your Community.*[16] His unique approach to evangelism is really about actions and not words. The actions are intended to spark conversation, and done while offering what is usually not free and nearly always a surprising kind of service. Servant Evangelism is not about hiding our light under a bushel, but it's also not about billboard advertising.

A couple of examples from Sjogren's book will help communicate the basic idea here. Envision, just for example, that a church has what he calls a "totally free car wash." That means there are signs up that it's free and the sign says "free car wash—no kidding." In addition to washing the cars, it is important to provide nice chairs, maybe offer some music, and give them

---

[16] Steve Sjogren, *101 Ways to Reach Your Community.* Colorado Springs, CO: Nav Poress, 2001.

a cup of coffee or a can of pop. It wouldn't hurt if someone were there from the church to actually answer any questions that someone might have.

A Christian group on a college campus can make a point on the day that freshmen are arriving by offering to help unload cars. They simply hand a small calling card to each new freshman, inviting them to some party or dinner that's being held. The same card will list the times that they gather for worship or prayer.

There is also the concept of *Pay It Forward*. The next time you're at Starbucks, for example, offer to buy coffee for the person who's behind you in line, and maybe then hand them a card that says a gift in God's name from the church that you serve.

What is common in all of these approaches to evangelism is that they involve a kind of gift giving and they open the door to conversations. It's not about being persuasive but about being invitational.

So You Never Want to Knock on Someone's Door if They Aren't Expecting You!

Here at the very end there's a little wiggle room left if the idea of knocking on doors in your neighborhood is still beyond belief—or maybe beyond your courage level. By this point, however, you may be intrigued by the basic idea that a great many people can become friends to your church, can know about it, and maybe even show up just to see what it is all about. Is there another way, one that is personal, and isn't costly, that can do the same? The answer is "Yes."

It goes back to that suggestion in the Dos and *Don'ts of Door-to-Door Ministry* (Chapter 5) where I talked about wearing a nametag. There are some pastors who have figured out that simply being known in the community as a pastor isn't enough. Episcopal clergy, for example, often wear distinctive black shirts with white collars. Some clergy carry a well-worn Bible. Some orthodox Jews will wear a black hat or a cap called a yarmulke. We all know that a person's clothing can make a religious statement, but that doesn't mean we engage them in conversation.

Remember the whole thrust of the ministry we've been discussing is about establishing relationships and making friends. Dress alone won't work. But a nametag can, if it's designed in a clever way, work to initiate a conversation.

I have found it extremely helpful in various pastorates that I have held to wear a small brass nametag—used with a strong magnet it attaches to a shirt pocket or the lapel of a sport coat. On it in clear block letters my name was printed and then below it the name of the church I served. It was the name of the church that usually stirred up the conversation. "What's an Episcopal church?" "Where's your church located?" "I think I attended a wedding there once." The first few times, I was surprised that my nametag elicited such a response, but then I learned to expect it to happen.

I also have some clergy friends who have taken this a step further, and I admire what they have done. They wear a distinctive appropriately casual shirt or blouse with the church name stenciled onto the lapel or pocket. It becomes part of their uniform, as it were, that they wear on a daily basis when they are working. Many of us in ministry have the freedom to meet people in many public places, and this means that we can invite many conversations with strangers. As I've noted before, the very idea of knocking on someone's door is extremely scary to some, but what if it is the strange who asks the first question? Well, if you follow my suggestions, it'll be a simple nametag that will lead to that question. And maybe to a new friend!

Chapter 9

God Gives the Growth

Some concluding thoughts on this ministry are in order. The spiritual and theological aspects of this ministry need to be brought back into focus after all the practical aspects have been discussed. When door-to-door ministry or Event Evangelism is rooted in prayer and faithfulness, those who participate will discover a whole series of blessings taking place in their lives. God works through this ministry. New friends in Christ will be made and many others will be grateful for this ministry. There are members in our congregations who will be encouraged to practice their own form of invitational ministry without even intending to be officially involved. It happens this way because it becomes part of the spirit of the faith community.

How all these blessings take place is certainly part of God's mystery in this process, but without a doubt, those who practice this ministry will experience signs of God's presence. One way to understand door-to-door ministry is to see it as a kind of seed-planting ministry. We should not judge it solely in terms of its immediate results. It is a ministry related to God's harvest, and as Paul noted, God does the harvesting after we have done our work. Writing to the church in Corinth with their factious divisions, Paul reminded them of the difference between his ministry, the ministry of Apollos, and the work of God. Paul said, "I planted, Apollos watered, but God gave the growth." (1 Cor. 3:6)

The truth of this harvest principle was underlined for me in a conversation I had with a well-known leader in the church-growth movement. This particular pastor started a couple of different churches using door-to-door ministry, before he became a teacher and a consultant. Some years later, he was asked to preach at an anniversary service of the first church he started. He'd been gone from this church for over 15 years. This pastor told me about a woman and her grown daughter who came up to him after the service. The woman said, "You may not remember me, but you stopped at our house years ago when you started this church. At the time I wasn't interested and didn't think I needed a church. Then my daughter was in an accident and I called one of the pastors at the church. You were gone by then. But since that time, I haven't missed church. I committed my life to Christ. And my daughter who is with me has done the same. I've always thanked God that you called on me when you did." When the pastor concluded this story, he said, "You never know whom you will touch and how God will use us." The harvest really belongs to God.

Finding the way to God's house

This is a ministry connecting the life of the church to the homes where people dwell. I sometimes call this a *home-reaching ministry*. I pointed out earlier that door-to-door ministry is an invitational ministry based on a relational understanding of evangelism. The text of a 20th century hymn, called "I come with joy to meet my Lord,"[17] captures the essence of this ministry. The first stanza is:

I come with joy to meet my Lord,
forgiven, loved and free,
in awe and wonder to recall,
his life laid down for me.

---

[17] Hymn 304. *The Hymnal 1982*. New York: The Church Hymnal Corporation, 1982. Words by Brian Wren.

This is a wonderful text for this ministry because we are not really introducing ourselves, or even our church, to those we meet. If we find people who aren't part of a Christian community, our prayer is that they will be able to say these words with sincerity and faith someday. These words remind us, as faithful Christians, of our motivation in coming to worship God. As the next stanza reminds us, though, this worship is based in community.

I come with Christians far and near,
to find as all are fed,
the new community of love
in Christ's communion bread.

One of the important aspects of door-to-door ministry is that it serves to invite those who have been furthest from the community to know they will be welcomed. This ministry, moreover, is bound to find some very lonely people who may be most receptive to the invitation offered, even if as shy people they say little at first. Once again, we aren't selling our personalities or any particular programs of the church. We offer people the opportunity to meet Christ, who is present in the sacraments, in the fellowship, and in the teaching of the church.

As Christ breaks bread and bids us share,
each proud division ends.
The love that made us makes us one,
and strangers now are friends.

In recent years I have had the privilege of teaching many others about this ministry. Whenever possible, we have included a hands-on experience so that people could actually make some calls. By now I have made calls in a large variety of situations. I've called in a small town in Oregon where over 70% of the people were unchurched. I've called in a few wealthy suburbs where the houses are quite far apart. On a couple of occasions, I've called in an older part of a city where the houses are quite close together and no longer in the nice condition known to their original owners. I have called in areas with a high percentage of minority people and found the same number of prospects as I'm used to finding in a suburb. To be sure, most calling for the new church I served was done in a suburban setting, but that's because the diocese wanted to start a church in this setting. Much to our surprise, and as a result of my calling, we discovered great diversity in this suburb. The diversity crossed the lines of race, ethnicity, economic status, and religious orientation. Door-to-door ministry is one of the best ways to meet a wide variety of people living in the community. Looking back after years of calling, wonder of wonders, the make-up of the church looked like the real community that surrounded the church!

Sadly, there are some housing situations in which door-to-door calling won't work. It really isn't possible to do this kind of calling, for example, with those living in apartments. It is too bad this is the case, because so many living in apartments become disconnected from institutions like the church. Apartment dwellers without a church represent a significant evangelistic challenge to the church. But all isn't lost, as there is a way to meet people without knocking on their doors. The idea at the end of the chapter on the Dos and Don'ts (Chapter 5) contains a great way to meet people who might live in situations that preclude going door-to-door.

Another group of people who are difficult to reach are those who have vacation homes. In Minnesota, for example, many people have a cabin on a northern lake. These people leave town on many weekends and lose touch with the life of the church.

It is also difficult to do this kind of calling in some rural areas, but only because of the distance between some homes. Finally, there is one kind of housing where calls are sadly impossible. In some parts of the country there are houses built in what are called "gated communities." Guardhouses often stand at the entrance to these areas, limiting access to the area. The rules in most of these developments preclude the kind of calling suggested in this book. Many successful secular people are living a secluded life in which wealth shields them from the invitational ministry that could give them a life money can't buy.

Even as I acknowledge certain housing situations that preclude door-to-door ministry, I want to emphasize once again how this ministry turns strangers into friends. This doesn't usually happen, however, with the first meeting. As I noted earlier, the friendship process emerges over time as follow-up visits are made. When guided by God, I also believe the racial, ethnic, and economic divisions that are signs of sin in our society and in the church start to fade as a result of this ministry. With this ministry, all people we meet, no matter how different they may be from me, hear a word of welcome. This is a ministry seeking to end our so-called "proud divisions."

And thus with joy we meet our Lord.
His presence always near,
is in such friendship better known:
we see and praise him here.

This is also an apostolic ministry in the sense that we are sent to represent Christ. It helps to remember the insight of Luke, which was that *Jesus would be coming to all the places visited by those sent out in ministry.* Jesus sends out disciples, but welcomes back apostles. A vision of ministry from Matthew's Gospel is also appropriate. In the last parable in Matthew, we are told to look for Jesus in those who are in need. The list of different ministries suggested includes welcoming the stranger. The telling words of Jesus in the parable are "just as you did it to the least of these who are members of my family, you did it to me." (Matt. 25:40) It is fairly obvious how door-to-door ministry presents us many opportunities to look for Christ in the lives of those we meet.

Together met, together bound,
we'll go our different ways,
and as his people in the world,
we'll live and speak his praise.

As I close this book, my mind is drawn to all the wonderful people God has added to the life of the church through this ministry. I know others came long after I'd left. I'm still thankful to those who knew that I needed to start door-knocking, even though at the time I wasn't sure it was necessary. It was. It still is.

The phrase "together met, together bound" so eloquently describes what has happened in my life and the lives of those who have responded to the invitations offered through door-to-door ministry. We were once strangers, but now our lives are interconnected through the life of the church. We may leave on Sunday going our separate ways, but even so, our lives are bound together by our faith and life together in Christ. I can easily think of so many in the church whom I first met through this ministry. We met as strangers. Since then, we've become friends. More important, they have either met the Lord for the first time or have renewed a commitment made in previous years. It was God, not I, who gave the growth to their faith. And it is God who has blessed my life by those who have come.

I know those of you who have read this work and who are willing to follow its precepts will find your lives richly blessed in some marvelous and surprising ways. You are going to make some friends out of some strangers. Your worship life will be deeper and richer. The surprising grace of God will be leading you to all the places and the people where Jesus wants to come. The doors are waiting for you. There are people who need to hear the invitation. Go and plant the seeds. Remember: God does the harvesting.

God be with you now and always.

～

Appendix

Luke 9:1 - 10:17

New Revised Standard Version

The Mission of the Twelve

Then Jesus called the twelve together and gave them power and authority over all demons and to cure diseases, and he sent them out to proclaim the kingdom of God and to heal. He said to them, 'Take nothing for your journey, no staff, nor bag, nor bread, nor money—not even an extra tunic. Whatever house you enter, stay there, and leave from there. Wherever they do not welcome you, as you are leaving that town shake the dust off your feet as a testimony against them.' They departed and went through the villages, bringing the good news and curing diseases everywhere.

Herod's Perplexity

Now Herod the ruler heard about all that had taken place, and he was perplexed, because it was said by some that John had been raised from the dead, by some that Elijah had appeared, and by others that one of the ancient prophets had arisen. Herod said, 'John I beheaded; but who is this about whom I hear such things?' And he tried to see him.

Feeding the Five Thousand

On their return the apostles told Jesus all they had done. He took them with him and withdrew privately to a city called Bethsaida. When the crowds found out about it, they followed him; and he welcomed them, and spoke to them about the kingdom of God, and healed those who needed to be cured.

The day was drawing to a close, and the twelve came to him and said, 'Send the crowd away, so that they may go into the surrounding villages and countryside, to lodge and get provisions; for we are here in a deserted place.' But he said to them, 'You give them something to eat.' They said, 'We have no more than five loaves and two fish—unless we are to go and buy food for all these people.' For there were about five thousand men. And he said to his disciples, 'Make them sit down in groups of about fifty each.' They did so and made them all sit down. And taking the five loaves and the two fish, he looked up to heaven, and blessed and broke them, and gave them to the disciples to set before the crowd. And all ate and were filled. What was left over was gathered up, twelve baskets of broken pieces.

Peter's Declaration about Jesus

Once when Jesus was praying alone, with only the disciples near him, he asked them, 'Who do the crowds say that I am?' They answered, 'John the Baptist; but others, Elijah; and still others, that one of the ancient prophets has arisen.' He said to them, 'But who do you say that I am?' Peter answered, 'The Messiah of God.'

Jesus Foretells His Death and Resurrection

He sternly ordered and commanded them not to tell anyone, saying, 'The Son of Man must undergo great suffering, and be rejected by the elders, chief priests, and scribes, and be killed, and on the third day be raised.'

Then he said to them all, 'If any want to become my followers, let them deny themselves and take up their cross daily and follow me. For those who want to save their life will lose it, and those who lose their life for my sake will save it. What does it profit them if they gain the whole world, but lose or forfeit themselves? Those who are ashamed of me and of my words, of them the Son of Man will be ashamed when he comes in his glory and the glory of the Father and of the holy angels. But truly I tell you, there are some standing here who will not taste death before they see the kingdom of God.'

The Transfiguration

Now about eight days after these sayings Jesus took with him Peter and John and James, and went up on the mountain to pray. And while he was praying, the appearance of his face changed, and his clothes became dazzling white. Suddenly they saw two men, Moses and Elijah, talking to him. They appeared in glory and were speaking of his departure, which he was about to accomplish at Jerusalem. Now Peter and his companions were weighed down with sleep; but since they had stayed awake, they saw his glory and the two men who stood with him. Just as they were leaving him, Peter said to Jesus, 'Master, it is good for us to be here; let us make three dwellings, one for you, one for Moses, and one for Elijah'—not knowing what he said. While he was saying this, a cloud came and overshadowed them; and they were terrified as they entered the cloud. Then from the cloud came a voice that said, 'This is my Son, my Chosen; listen to him!' When the voice had spoken, Jesus was found alone. And they kept silent and in those days told no one any of the things they had seen.

Jesus Heals a Boy with a Demon

On the next day, when they had come down from the mountain, a great crowd met him. Just then a man from the crowd shouted, 'Teacher, I beg you to look at my son; he is my only child. Suddenly a spirit seizes him, and all at once he shrieks. It throws him into convulsions until he foams at the mouth; it mauls him and will scarcely leave him. I begged your disciples to cast it out, but they could not.' Jesus answered, 'You faithless and perverse generation, how much longer must I be with you and bear with you? Bring your son here.' While he was coming, the demon dashed him to the ground in convulsions. But Jesus rebuked the unclean spirit, healed the boy, and gave him back to his father. And all were astounded at the greatness of God.

Jesus Again Foretells His Death

While everyone was amazed at all that he was doing, he said to his disciples, 'Let these words sink into your ears: The Son of Man is going to be betrayed into human hands.' But they did not understand this saying; its meaning was concealed from them, so that they could not perceive it. And they were afraid to ask him about this saying.

True Greatness

An argument arose among them as to which one of them was the greatest. But Jesus, aware of their inner thoughts, took a little child and put it by his side, and said to them, 'Whoever welcomes this child in my name welcomes me, and whoever welcomes me welcomes the one who sent me; for the least among all of you is the greatest.'

Another Exorcist

John answered, 'Master, we saw someone casting out demons in your name, and we tried to stop him, because he does not follow with us.' But Jesus said to him, 'Do not stop him; for whoever is not against you is for you.'

A Samaritan Village Refuses to Receive Jesus

When the days drew near for him to be taken up, he set his face to go to Jerusalem. And he sent messengers ahead of him. On their way they entered a village of the Samaritans to make ready for him; but they did not receive him, because his face was set towards Jerusalem. When his disciples James and John saw it, they said, 'Lord, do you want us to command fire to come down from heaven and consume them?' But he turned and rebuked them. Then they went on to another village.

Would-Be Followers of Jesus

As they were going along the road, someone said to him, 'I will follow you wherever you go.' And Jesus said to him, 'Foxes have holes, and birds of the air have nests; but the Son of Man has nowhere to lay his head.' To another he said, 'Follow me.' But he said, 'Lord, first let me go and bury my father.' But Jesus said to him, 'Let the dead bury their own dead; but as for you, go and proclaim the kingdom of God.' Another said, 'I will follow you, Lord; but let me first say farewell to those at my home.' Jesus said to him, 'No one who puts a hand to the plough and looks back is fit for the kingdom of God.'

The Mission of the Seventy

After this the Lord appointed seventy others and sent them on ahead of him in pairs to every town and place where he himself intended to go. He said to them, 'The harvest is plentiful, but the labourers are few; therefore ask the Lord of the harvest to send out labourers into his harvest. Go on your way. See, I am sending you out like lambs into the midst of wolves. Carry no purse, no bag, no sandals; and greet no one on the road. Whatever house you enter, first say, "Peace to this house!" And if anyone is there who shares in peace, your peace will rest on that person; but if not, it will return to you. Remain in the same house, eating and drinking whatever they provide, for the labourer deserves to be paid. Do not move about from house to house. Whenever you enter a town and its people welcome you, eat what is set before you; cure the sick who are there, and say to them, "The kingdom of God has come near to you." But whenever you enter a town and they do not welcome you, go out into its streets and say, "Even the dust of your town that clings to our feet, we wipe off in protest against you. Yet know this: the kingdom of God has come near." I tell you, on that day it will be more tolerable for Sodom than for that town.

Woes to Unrepentant Cities

'Woe to you, Chorazin! Woe to you, Bethsaida! For if the deeds of power done in you had been done in Tyre and Sidon, they would have repented long ago, sitting in sackcloth and ashes. But at the judgement it will be more tolerable for Tyre and Sidon than for you. And you, Capernaum, will you be exalted to heaven?

No, you will be brought down to Hades.

'Whoever listens to you listens to me, and whoever rejects you rejects me, and whoever rejects me rejects the one who sent me.'

The Return of the Seventy

The seventy returned with joy, saying, 'Lord, in your name even the demons submit to us!"

Acknowledgments

There are a great many people I want to thank as I conclude the writing of this teaching book. There were many wonderful friends who encouraged and supported me when I started the work of planting a new Episcopal church in the summer of 1986. I am humbled when I think of the early days in our new church life as a time when I was most reluctant to go out calling door-to-door. There were two people, however, who were instrumental in helping give me the courage to make those first calls. One of those people was Skidmore Olson, a member of the Diocesan new church committee, who kept asking me month after month when I was going to start calling. I had lots of excuses for a long time. I thank him for his perseverance and his encouragement. Skidmore passed on, but I know that he saw those pearly gates open. I suspect he hangs out near those gates, welcoming others.

The other person who helped me is my brother pastor and friend, The Rev. Larry Smith, who was starting a Lutheran church at the same time. Larry was out making calls as a way to start his church and he served as my mentor during my first few months when I started calling.

I'm grateful for the clergy and laypeople who have attended a variety of seminars and listened to a number of different talks on this subject over the past few years. The first workshop on door-to-door ministry was conducted in the Diocese of Chicago. This material was presented to a clergy conference in the Diocese of Minnesota. Hundreds more through 20+ years have attended "Start Up! Start Over!" a church-growth seminar sponsored by the national Episcopal Church. At this conference, I was always speaking about evangelism and never failed to tell them, even if their ears were closed, about this ministry.

With e-book publishing, the story of all that I've learned in door-to-door ministry continued in 2012 when the Kindle version of this book was published. I was pleased to be able to add many new ideas and a deeper explanation of things in that format. The essentials about door-to-door ministry were there, but what I've been able to include many suggestions for welcoming people that have to do with the main door to the church itself. I am pleased that I've been able to get this in print, because I know that there will be evangelism groups and classes in seminaries that can make use of this work.

I want to thank The Rev. Frank Logue for his encouragement to get this book printed. Having in this format makes is accessible to small groups in a church. I'm grateful to my son-in-law Manny Fimbres, a very talented graphic artist, for the cover.

The task of writing requires a special kind of discipline, some creativity, and attention to detail. The latter factor is my Achilles heel. There would be a great many grammatical problems in this book without the help of Cheryl Crockett, my editor. I am responsible for what has been published and whatever errors there are, but ever so grateful for her help in this process.

I want any church that wants to invite me to help them with a day of calling to know that I'm just a phone call away. I'd love to help you reach your neighbors!

Faithfully in Christ,
The Rev. Dr. George H. Martin
P.S. You can reach me at my website: www.georgemartin.org

Contacting the Author

If you would like to talk to me about any questions you might have please use the contact information found on this page to reach me. I welcome the opportunity to hear from you. I am available to come to your church or area to conduct a training event on this particular method of reaching people, as well as with a number of other tools needed for reaching people with the Good News!

The Rev. Dr. George H. Martin
www.georgemartin.org

ISBN: 978-1-4675-3879-4

INDEX

Made in the USA
San Bernardino, CA
27 July 2014